A Practical Guide to Teaching Music in the Secondary School

A Practical Guide to Teaching Music in the Secondary School provides valuable support, guidance and creative ideas for student teachers, mentors and practising teachers who want to develop their music teaching. Written to accompany the successful textbook *Learning to Teach Music in the Secondary School*, it will help you understand important current developments and explore new possibilities for teaching and learning.

Focusing on teaching music *musically*, the book explores musical learning through placing pupils at the centre of a musical experience. Considering the revised KS3 curriculum and the 14–19 agenda in music, it also seeks to broaden the perspectives of music teachers through engaging with collaborative practice, transitions and cross-curricular work. Key issues explored include:

- personalising musical learning;
- teaching creatively and promoting creativity;
- approaches to using ICT in the classroom;
- musical collaboration with other adults;
- assessment for learning in music;
- making connections with other subjects.

Using practical examples and tasks, this book will help you critically examine the way in which children learn music. It is an invaluable resource for those involved in teaching music who are seeking to develop their practical and theoretical understanding.

Julie Evans is Senior Lecturer in Music Education at Canterbury Christ Church University. She has been a music teacher and head of music in five secondary schools as well as an instrumental teacher of violin and piano.

Chris Philpott is Head of the Department of Secondary Education at the University of Greenwich and has been responsible for Secondary PGCE music programmes in two universities.

Routledge Teaching Guides
Series Editors: Susan Capel and Marilyn Leask

These Practical Guides have been designed as companions to **Learning to Teach [Subject] in the Secondary School.** For further information on the Routledge Teaching Guides series please visit our website at www.routledge.com/education

Other titles in this series

A Practical Guide to Teaching Physical Education in the Secondary School
Edited by Susan Capel, Peter Breckon and Jean O'Neill

A Practical Guide to Teaching Modern Foreign Languages in the Secondary School
Edited by Norbert Pachler and Ana Redondo

A Practical Guide to Teaching Citizenship in the Secondary School
Edited by Liam Gearon

A Practical Guide to Teaching ICT in the Secondary School
Steve Kennewell

A Practical Guide to Teaching Design and Technology in the Secondary School
Edited by Gwyneth Owen-Jackson

A Practical Guide to Teaching History in the Secondary School
Edited by Martin Hunt

A Practical Guide to Teaching Science in the Secondary School
Douglas P. Newton

A Practical Guide to Teaching Music in the Secondary School

Edited by
Julie Evans and Chris Philpott

Routledge
Taylor & Francis Group

LONDON AND NEW YORK

First published 2009
by Routledge
2 Park Square, Milton Park, Abingdon, Oxon OX14 4RN

Simultaneously published in the USA and Canada
by Routledge
270 Madison Avenue, New York, NY 10016

Routledge is an imprint of the Taylor & Francis Group, an informa business

Typeset in Palatino and Frutiger by
Keystroke, 28 High Street, Tettenhall, Wolverhampton
Printed and bound in Great Britain by
MPG Books Group, UK

British Library Cataloguing in Publication Data
A catalogue record for this book is available from the British Library

Library of Congress Cataloging in Publication Data
A practical guide to teaching music in the secondary school / edited by
Julie Evans and Chris Philpott.
p. cm. – (Routledge teaching guides)
Includes bibliographical references and index.
1. School music–Instruction and study–Great Britain. I. Evans, Julie, 1958–
II. Philpott, Chris, 1956–
MT3.G7P65 2009
780.71′2–dc22
2008047800

ISBN 10: 0–415–48258–5 (pbk)
ISBN 10: 0–203–87799–3 (ebk)

ISBN 13: 978–0–415–48258–5 (pbk)
ISBN 13: 978–0–203–87799–9 (ebk)

Contents

List of figures and tables

FIGURES

TABLES

Contributors

Jonathan Barnes is Senior Lecturer in Education at Canterbury Christ Church University. He has wide experience in all sectors of education. He now teaches a range of disciplines in teacher education, music, art, geography and history. His research is in the relationships between the curriculum, creativity and well-being. He writes regularly on cross-curricular and creative approaches to the curriculum and staff development.

Julie Evans has been a music teacher and head of department in five secondary schools. She has also had extensive experience as an instrumental teacher of both violin and piano. She is currently a Senior Lecturer in Music Education at Canterbury Christ Church University where she is responsible for the 11–18 and 7–14 Postgraduate Certificate in Education (PGCE) Music courses.

Keith Evans is Senior Lecturer in Music Education at the University of Greenwich where he coordinates the Secondary PGCE Musicians in Education course in collaboration with Trinity College of Music. He previously taught music in a number of schools in Kent, latterly in a specialist music school.

Martin Fautley is Reader in Music Education at Birmingham City University, where he teaches on the Secondary PGCE and research programmes. For many years he was a secondary school music teacher, subsequently undertaking doctoral research into the teaching, learning and assessment of creative acts in music in the classroom. His published work lies mainly in the areas of teaching and learning composing, and on assessment in music education.

John Finney is Senior Lecturer in Music Education in the Faculty of Education, University of Cambridge. He teaches on undergraduate and higher degree programmes with special responsibility for preparing graduates to teach music in secondary schools. His current research examines pupils' perspectives on their musical experiences in secondary schools, their potential for designing curricula and taking leadership roles within the music classroom. At the same time he is researching the evolution of progressive ideas within music education 1950 to the present day.

Duncan Mackrill is Senior Lecturer in Music Education at the University of Sussex where he is also the PGCE Convenor. Previously he gained many years' experience as a secondary head of music and a music technology education consultant. His interests include integrating and developing ICT in music education, ePortfolios and Virtual Learning Environments. In September 2005 he was awarded a National Teaching Fellowship by the Higher Education Academy.

Chris Philpott taught music and performing arts in secondary schools for 16 years before moving into teacher education as a PGCE tutor and programme director. His writing is mainly in the field of music education but he has also published on mentoring. He is currently Head of the Department of Secondary Education at the University of

Greenwich where the Music PGCE includes an innovative collaboration with Trinity College of Music.

Ian Shirley is Senior Lecturer in Primary Music Education at Edge Hill University. He is joint editor of *Primary Music Today* and an active member of the national choral organisation, Sing for Pleasure. He was the project manager of HEARTS (Higher Education, Arts and Schools) at Canterbury Christ Church University and has written about the impact of an arts-based curriculum on student teachers' development.

Gary Spruce is Senior Lecturer in Education at the Open University. His primary responsibility is as subject leader for the University's flexible PGCE music course. He has written widely on music education and presented papers at national and international conferences. He is a practising musician with a particular interest in music for the theatre.

Katherine Zeserson is responsible for the strategic design, direction and implementation of the Sage Gateshead's internationally acclaimed Learning and Participation programme. She has a national reputation as a trainer and music educator in a wide range of community, educational and social contexts including pre-school settings, primary and secondary classrooms, voluntary sector organisations, higher and further education postgraduate and professional training programmes. She has held many arts-in-education residencies, working with both primary and secondary age children.

Series editors' introduction

This practical and accessible work book is part of a series of textbooks for student teachers within the Routledge Teaching Guides Series. It complements and extends the popular textbook entitled *Learning to Teach in the Secondary School: A Companion to School Experience*, as well as the subject-specific book *Learning to Teach Music in the Secondary School*. We anticipate that you will want to use this book in conjunction with these other books.

Teaching is rapidly becoming a more research- and evidence-informed profession. We have used research and professional evidence about what makes good practice to underpin the Routledge Teaching Guides Series and these practical workbooks. Both the generic and subject-specific books in the series provide theoretical, research and professional evidence-based advice and guidance to support you as you focus on developing aspects of your teaching or your pupils' learning as you progress through your initial teacher education course and beyond. Although the generic and subject-specific books include some case studies and tasks to help you consider the issues, the practical application of material is not their major focus. That is the role of this book.

This book aims to reinforce your understanding of aspects of your teaching, support you in aspects of your development as a teacher and your teaching, and enable you to analyse your success as a teacher in maximising pupils' learning by focusing on practical applications. The practical activities in this book may be used in a number of ways. Some activities are designed to be undertaken by you individually, others as a joint task in pairs and yet others as group work working with, for example, other student teachers or a school- or university-based tutor. Your tutor may use the activities with a group of student teachers. The book has been designed so that you can write directly into it.

In England, new ways of working for teachers are being developed through an initiative remodelling the school workforce. This may mean that you have a range of colleagues to support in your classroom. They also provide an additional resource on which you can draw. In any case, you will, of course, need to draw on additional resources to support your development and the *Learning to Teach in the Secondary School*, 5th edn website (http://www.routledge.com/textbooks/9780415478724) which lists key websites for Scotland, Wales, Northern Ireland and England. For example, key websites relevant to teachers in England include the Teacher Training Resource Bank (www.ttrb.ac.uk). Others include: www.teachernet.gov.uk, which is part of the DfES schools web initiative; www.becta.org.uk, which contains ICT resources; and www.qca.org.uk, which is the Qualifications and Curriculum Authority website.

We do hope that this practical workbook is useful in supporting your development as a teacher. We welcome feedback which can be incorporated into future editions.

Susan Capel
Marilyn Leask
February 2009

Introduction

JULIE EVANS AND CHRIS PHILPOTT

This practical guide complements the successful textbook *Learning to Teach Music in the Secondary School* by Chris Philpott and Gary Spruce (2007), also published by Routledge. The book is intended to support student teachers who are learning to teach music in a wide range of contexts, along with their higher education and school-based tutors and mentors. It brings together work by a wide range of professionals who are engaged with teacher education. It provides a range of practical activities designed to support student teachers' development in music teaching and their understanding of important current developments within and beyond the curriculum. The book will also allow experienced music teachers to consider how they might develop their practice in line with these important developments, challenging them to explore new possibilities.

Each chapter includes:

- an explicit statement about the objectives;
- a detailed discussion of the relevant issues and concepts;
- a series of practical tasks which allow exploration of the material in a range of contexts;
- suggestions for further reading aiming to deepen knowledge in each of the areas covered.

The first two chapters give suggestions as to the nature of personalised learning in the secondary music classroom at Key Stage 3 and in 14–19 education. Some chapters explicitly consider the principles of the revised National Curriculum for Music including topics such as:

- cultural understanding
- critical thinking and understanding
- creativity and creative teaching.

Other chapters are intended to deepen understanding of topics which have had a significant impact on music education in recent years, such as:

- developing the integration of ICT in the music classroom;
- developing assessment for learning in the music classroom;
- collaboration between music teachers and other professionals.

The remaining chapters consider perennial issues which are currently in the forefront of discussion in music education because of a raft of recent initiatives:

- continuing your pupils' experiences of singing and instrumental learning from Key Stage 2 to Key Stage 3;
- the integration of practice both within music and between music and other subjects.

The book is intended to challenge both students and experienced teachers to explore possibilities in musical learning. It also intends to engage them in critical reflection on practice as a basis for becoming more effective music teachers.

In conclusion, the book is based upon some important principles which we believe to underpin effective practice in the twenty-first century. First, that music needs to be taught musically by placing pupils at the centre of a musical experience in the school. Second, that learning for pupils needs be personalised through taking into account the musical understandings that they bring with them. Finally, that music in the school should aim to provide access and achievement for all pupils.

Part 1 Musical learning

Chapter 1   Personalising learning in music education

CHRIS PHILPOTT

INTRODUCTION

The personalisation of learning is a major theme in current education policy and is the most recent manifestation of an ongoing concern for individual needs and inclusion, i.e. a concern to engage pupils in learning and to provide access to achievement for all.

The personalisation of learning has long been an important issue in music education and in many ways the past 50 years of curriculum developments have been targeted at inclusion. For example, there has been an awareness that while 'music' is an important part of the lives of most pupils, their engagement and achievements in 'school music' has been limited to a relatively small elite. Developments in music education such as an increased emphasis on composition, 'world' musics, 'pop' music, technology and, most recently, the use of 'informal' pedagogies have been inspired, at least in part, by a desire for a more inclusive music curriculum.

There is a sense in which the whole of this book is about how to personalise the learning for your pupils. Each chapter aims to develop your understanding of how to maximise the musical engagement and achievements for all.

OBJECTIVES

By the end of this chapter you should be able to:

- understand what personalisation means in music education;
- understand how some current initiatives in music education articulate with personalisation;
- devise some strategies for personalising learning in music.

PERSONALISING LEARNING

What is meant by personalisation? What is meant by the personalisation of learning in the music classroom?

Christine Gilbert has defined personalising learning as 'focusing . . . on each child's learning in order to enhance progress, achievement and participation' (DfES 2006b: 3).

To realise this aim Hargreaves (2006) has identified nine interconnected 'gateways' to personalisation and these 'gateways' resonate with many of the chapters in this book. The 'gateways' represent a way of conceptualising the strategies to maximise achievements for all pupils and for them to achieve their potential.

Reading Box 1.1 and carrying out Tasks 1.1 and 1.2 will enable you to audit your own experience and ideas in relation to the gateways.

Box 1.1 Nine gateways to personalisation

Assessment for learning (AfL)

AfL is about teachers and pupils coming to know themselves and each other through, for example, questioning and feedback. AfL is embedded in teaching and learning such that it can feed forward into how and what to learn and thus contribute to personalisation.

Learning to learn

Learning to learn is about pupils developing the skills to take control of their own learning. The notion implies the development of a metacognitive awareness of the learning process that leads to an increased independence from teacher-led learning.

Student (pupil) voice

When the pupil's voice contributes to personalisation pupils are invited to make a contribution to, for example, the organisation of the curriculum and the school. The concept of co-construction is important here.

Curriculum

Personalisation of the curriculum is not only about choice (of subject, of syllabus), but also about promoting approaches to teaching and learning which facilitate real engagement, e.g. planning for creativity and the pupil voice.

New technologies

Technologies can enhance personalisation through their capacity to provide alternative teaching strategies and a wide range of resources. They can also provide access, control and independence in learning.

School design and organisation

Schools can be designed and organised to maximise personalisation. This could involve devising a timetable to maximise curriculum choice or designing classrooms to facilitate a flexible approach to learning.

Advice and guidance

Personalising learning will require pupils to be able to make informed choices about their micro and macro progress. This guidance might come from a wide variety of sources both within and outside of the school.

Mentoring and coaching

Mentoring and coaching involves more targeted and ongoing support for learning. Such support can come in the form of pupil to pupil or adult to pupil. The adult can come from within the school or from the wider community.

Workforce development

Personalised learning can be supported through the deployment of a wide range of professionals. For example, there are an increasing number of 'para-professionals' who engage with pupils, such as teaching assistants and community workers.

Task 1.1 Auditing experience and ideas on the personalisation of learning

Gateway	What have you experienced as a learner?	What have you observed in placement schools?	What are the implications for music education?	Where else in this book will you find support?
Assessment for learning				
Learning to learn				
Student (pupil) voice				
Curriculum				
New technologies				
School design and organisation				
Advice and guidance				
Mentoring and coaching				
Workforce development				

Task 1.2 A presentation on one of the gateways

Take one of the gateways and devise a presentation on the implications for music education. Your research for the presentation should include current initiatives, e.g. the National Curriculum, Musical Futures, Music Manifesto, Wider Opportunities. Share this with your peers, either face to face or online, perhaps via a Virtual Learning Environment (VLE).

PERSONALISING LEARNING IN MUSIC

It is clear that the nine gateways are intimately related; for example, if pupils are given opportunities to choose which pieces they wish to perform they are engaging in the co-construction of the curriculum, exercising their 'voice' and there is the potential for an informed dialogue with their teachers (AfL). For this reason Hargreaves (2006) has clustered the nine gateways into 'deeps' which make the links between them more explicit. These 'deeps' are:

- deep learning – assessment for learning, student (pupil) voice, learning to learn;
- deep experience – curriculum, new technologies;
- deep support – mentoring and coaching, advice and guidance;
- deep leadership – design and organisation, workforce reform.

Given that 'deep learning' is a central aim of personalisation, the other 'deeps' can be seen as servicing this and Figure 1.1 illustrates the relationship between them.

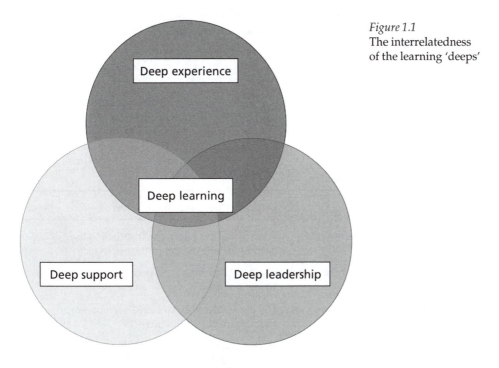

Figure 1.1
The interrelatedness
of the learning 'deeps'

In the rest of this chapter we will examine some case studies in personalisation with specific reference to music education. What do the personalised learning 'deeps' mean for music education? The 'deeps' imply access for all to a music curriculum with 'deep' musical learning at its centre, where pupils use music to make sense of their world, through creating, performing and listening to musical ideas.

CASE STUDIES OF THE 'DEEPS' IN MUSIC EDUCATION

The following case studies use several current initiatives to exemplify personalisation of learning although they are *not* a full exposition of the initiatives themselves, nor the possibilities within each 'deep'.

Deep learning: informal pedagogies

As part of the Paul Hamlyn funded Musical Futures project, Lucy Green (2001, 2008) has used her work on how pop musicians learn to research a classroom pedagogy which exploits informal learning processes, i.e. the processes that some popular musicians seem to employ when learning in music.

> Playing music of one's own choice, with which one identifies personally, operating both as a performer and a composer with like minded friends, and having fun doing it must be high priorities in the quest for increasing numbers of young people to benefit from a music education which makes music not merely available, but meaningful, worthwhile and participatory.
>
> (Green 2001: 16)

Part of the motivation for this work has been the often-found paradox that while music is so important in the lives of pupils, 'school music' is not! See Task 1.3.

Task 1.3 The music paradox

Do you think that the music paradox exists? If yes, then draw up a list of 'reasons' and 'remedies'. If no, then draw up a list of your evidence for this answer. Use the list as the basis of a group discussion or online discussion. You could also post a 'blog' on this issue on your VLE.

The model for informal pedagogy devised by the Musical Futures research team was based on five principles (see Green 2008: 9–10) and in Table 1.1 we can see the links to be made with 'deep learning'.

Table 1.1 Musical Futures and deep learning

Musical Futures principles	Links with 'deep learning'
Pupils work with music chosen by themselves that they enjoy and identify with	This exemplifies pupils co-constructing the curriculum and the use of the pupil voice
Pupils work in the main aurally through listening and copying	Pupils engage in self and peer feedback, a central strategy in AfL
Pupils work with peers in groups chosen by themselves	The pupil voice is again heard here (as almost everywhere else in this project)
Skills and knowledge are gained in a rather haphazard fashion with whole 'real' pieces at the core	Here the pupils are learning to learn, i.e. they will understand that learning is not always linear or broken into small chunks
Listening, performing and composing are integrated throughout the learning process	Again they learn something about learning, i.e. that it can be holistic and is full of connections

As a result of their research the Musical Futures team have devised an approach to informal pedagogy and informal learning in the classroom which aims to stimulate greater motivation and achievement for pupils (see www.musicalfutures.org).

Crucial to developing your own approach to informal pedagogy in the classroom is understanding your role as a teacher. Informal pedagogy draws upon and promotes informal learning and thus aims to begin with the musical ideas and knowledge of the pupils themselves. The role of the 'teacher' in the learning process can be relatively non-interventionist where teachers are seen as facilitators of learning, a resource for the pupils to draw on. These 'new' relationships between pupil–pupil, pupil–teacher and teacher–teacher are key to militating against pupil alienation from school music. There is real ownership of the music and a personalisation of the musical learning; deep learning. As student teachers in music it is important that you begin to explore the notion of informal pedagogy and learning, and Task 1.4 will help you to do this.

The use of informal pedagogy and learning for personalisation can present many challenges to the practice of music education in schools, for example, in the context of a statutory National Curriculum for Music.

Task 1.4 Living informal learning

1 As part of your initial teacher education (ITE) you will have carried out an audit of your subject knowledge. Once again, with a group of peers, decide how your collective 'points for development' can be addressed through collaborative peer learning. What areas for development can be addressed in this way? How can you go about supporting each other?

2 Use Table 1.1 as a template to audit your own engagement with informal pedagogy and learning as part of your own musical development. How important have these 'principles' been in your own music education at different times in your musical life thus far? Share these with your peers.

Deep experience: the National Curriculum for Music

A 'new' KS3 National Curriculum for Music was published in 2007. This section will not 'case study' the music-specific content found in the Programmes of Study which are taken up in other chapters, e.g. critical thinking and cultural understanding. We focus here on a set of underpinning aims and skills for all subjects.

The logo of the new curriculum is a series of intertwining coloured lines which represent the interconnectedness of subjects and their contribution to the education of the whole child. The new curriculum aims to provide 'deep experience' by making significant connections between areas of human experience.

Music is expected to contribute to the whole child in the following ways:

- through cross-curricular dimensions
- through personal development
- through the development of skills.

Box 1.2 offers a further explanation of what is meant by each of these. Task 1.5 follows on from Box 1.2.

Box 1.2 National Curriculum for Music: contributing to the whole child

Cross-curricular dimensions

- identity and cultural diversity
- healthy lifestyles
- community participation
- enterprise
- global dimension and sustainable development
- technology and the media
- creativity and critical thinking.

Personal development

Every Child Matters includes:
- be healthy
- stay safe

Box 1.2 *continued*

- enjoy and achieve
- make a positive contribution
- achieve economic well-being.

Skills

Functional skills:
- English
- Maths
- ICT.

Personal, learning and thinking skills (PLTS):
- independent enquirers
- creative thinkers
- reflective learners
- team workers
- self-managers
- effective participators.

Task 1.5 Deep experience and the National Curriculum

1 Using Box 1.2, create a table which audits the contribution that learning in music can contribute to each. Use this table as the basis for a discussion about the role of music in 'deep experience'.
2 In what ways are the elements in Box 1.2 themselves interconnected? Draw lines of connection between them and be prepared to explain your 'lines'.
3 In what ways are these elements connected with the main programme of study for music? Annotate Box 1.2.

The new National Curriculum aims to give schools the flexibility and autonomy to organise the curriculum such that the emphasis on connections and the whole child can be achieved (see http://qca.org.uk). How can the school curriculum be organised to make deep connections and provide deep experience? For example, in some primary schools the curriculum is often integrated, i.e. topic based, involving a wide range of subjects. Does such work have a role in the secondary school? An increasing number of secondary schools *are* introducing more integrated, topic-based work especially in years 7 and 8. In some of the more innovative curricula the PLTS are the focus of timetabled sessions and not the subjects. The 'new' National Curriculum is concerned with the motivation of pupils and it is felt that deep experience is the key to a lifelong and personalised engagement with learning. Now carry out Task 1.6.

The new National Curriculum for Music aims to contribute to the deep experience, and thus the deep personalised learning of pupils, through making connections with and between the themes which underpin all subjects.

Task 1.6 Organising the curriculum for deep experience

1 In what ways might curriculum time and organisation of the subjects be adapted to achieve the aims of making connections and educating the whole child? Draw up a possible timetable for one week in the life of a year 7 class as a solution to share with your peers.
2 Start an online debate with your peers on the question: what is the relative importance of the subject (music) and the wider aims of educating the whole child? Does the National Curriculum compromise the integrity of music in the curriculum?
3 Take one of the categories in Box 1.1 and compare this with the principles of 'Musical Futures'. Is there any relationship? Once you have done this, answer the question: how can informal learning and pedagogy help to achieve the underlying aims of the National Curriculum?

Deep support: talented musicians

Pupils have many individual needs in the music classroom, e.g. gender, disability, culture and deep support can be targeted at these needs to enhance deep experience and deep learning. As a case study for deep support this section will examine how a specific individual need can benefit from advice, guidance, mentoring and coaching, i.e. the case of the 'talented' musical learner.

While this is not the place to undertake a critique of the concept of 'talented' it is clear that some learners in music have outstanding abilities. When addressing talented pupils in music it is worth making the following points:

1 Musical learning is for all pupils and all pupils are musical.
2 Musical talent is on a continuum and should not be constructed as a dichotomy of 'musical' or 'not musical'.
3 A particular talent can be observed in, or emerge at, any stage of development; talent can also be latent.
4 Talent might show up in any aspect of music-making, e.g. composition, performance.
5 Talent can be nurtured in all styles and traditions of music.

However, before we can offer deep support to our pupils, we need to be able to recognise those who have 'talent'. Talented learners in music might demonstrate several of the following:

- they can memorise music quickly;
- they can imitate music with ease;
- they can sing and/or play with a natural awareness of musical expression;
- they have a strong desire to communicate through music;
- they have a strong response to music, e.g. physically;
- they have an affinity to a musical instrument and/or their voice;
- they have a powerful creative impulse;
- they show high levels of motivation and independence in their musical learning.

Support for the talented learner in music needs to be handled sensitively. For example, there is increasing evidence that pupils are most motivated when they have a degree of autonomy in their learning. It is not that pupils do not need support or that they do not want it, but that they must be ready and receptive for it to have an impact. When and how to intervene are part of the professional skills developed by the music teacher.

For this reason the music teacher should learn to gauge *if* to intervene, *when* to intervene and *how* to intervene. The process outlined in Box 1.3 is useful for addressing the needs of the talented learner in music. There is no right or wrong here; only a professional judgement about appropriate intervention. After reading Box 1.3 carry out Task 1.7.

Box 1.3 Four scenarios of talented learners in music

Scenario 1

Adi is in year 9 and is a self-taught guitarist. He is the driving force behind a rock band of pupils in his year who mainly compose their own music, to which he is fiercely committed. Although a relatively limited guitarist, he is able to use the chords and techniques; he does know how to pastiche and compose with great originality. He will also have a go at improvising freely if he has half a chance and he sings with style and power in the rock idiom.

Scenario 2

Jane is in year 8 and plays cornet in a first section brass band; she has recently been promoted to the solo cornet rank. Jane has cornet lessons with a trumpet teacher from the local music service. She has a bright and forthright sound and good technical ability which she uses in the full range of styles played by the band, from pop arrangements to musicals to dedicated brass band music. Jane focuses on developing her performing skills.

Scenario 3

Wes is in year 7 and in some of the class drumming workshops he has shown a really tight sense of pulse on the congas. Furthermore, he is able to weave some intricate improvisations around the basic beat and maintain some complex polyrhythm. He also uses his singing voice with great verve, expression and good tuning and is unafraid to 'solo'. Wes enjoys music lessons especially when they give him opportunities to perform.

Scenario 4

Sally is in year 10 and is devoted to the programme 'Reason'. She has this software on her computer at home and also works on it at school. Sally's music is most frequently influenced by drum and bass/jungle style to which she is hugely committed, and yet her work shows high levels of originality. She is working for her General Certificate of Secondary Education (GCSE) and will use her compositions as part of the coursework.

Aspects of available support

People available for deep support: teachers, instrumental teachers, local community musicians (e.g. local band), teaching assistants, other pupils, other teachers (e.g. careers), outside agencies (e.g. music services, library), parents, the individual pupils themselves.

Roles in deep support (while all of these roles overlap we can make some distinctions):

- teaching: taking an overarching view of learning in school music;
- mentoring: (in this sense) taking part in mutually agreed support for learning;

Box 1.3 *continued*

- coaching: passing on and supporting the learning of, for example, a specific set of skills and knowledge;
- advising and guiding: focusing on the opportunities for learning available.

Strategies which can be employed: talented pupils supporting other pupils (and thus supporting themselves), providing challenge, teaching input, setting high expectations, challenging through ICT, developing rich resources, extension activities, enrichment activities (e.g. outside of class), open-ended problem solving, independent study, research, others?

Task 1.7 Deep support for talented musicians

For each of the scenarios in Box 1.3, devise some potential deep support for the pupils (assuming it is appropriate) in order to promote their deep experience and deep learning. Which people could be involved? What role(s) might they take on? What strategies could they use? Write some bullet points for each scenario and share them with your peers. What similarities and distinctions do you notice and what issues arise?

There is a danger that talented pupils can be pushed too hard and this can be perceived by them to be unfair. However, problems can also occur when pupils underachieve, for example, when talented pupils are not motivated or challenged poor behaviour can result and become a real barrier to further progress. The perceptive and sensitive use of a range of strategies is thus important when producing deep support for pupils.

Deep leadership: designing a music department

Part of such leadership for personalisation is the design and organisation of the school. As a case study for deep leadership we will examine the development of an ideal facility to promote deep experience, support and learning, i.e. the music department itself.

The government scheme called Building Schools for the Future (BSF) aims to refurbish old schools and build new ones. There are two reasons for the existence of the scheme, first, that many schools are getting old, and second, there is a need to rethink what places of learning might look like, especially in light of the personalisation agenda. The scheme represents an opportunity for teachers and pupils to be a part of designing schools that are fit for twenty-first-century learning. However, personalisation does not only imply rethinking school design, but also brings into question the way that schools have been traditionally organised. Naturally, as part of this work, the design and organisation of music departments is also being scrutinised.

Box 1.4 contains an inventory of a typical secondary music department; read this and carry out Task 1.8.

The BSF scheme invites a creative response when designing and remodelling schools. There is an opportunity for headteachers to lead on an educational vision, and to put this vision into the shape and organisation of the school. For example, some schools have been designed with large open-plan 'learning plazas' (with few traditional classrooms). Lessons

---

Box 1.4 The secondary school music department

The typical secondary music department might include:

- one or two main teaching rooms with a keyboard, sound equipment with one possibly set up with music-related ICT equipment (computers and/or electronic keyboards);
- a number of small practice rooms (often used by instrumental teachers);
- a store room;
- a collection of orchestral instruments, 'world music' instruments, classroom instruments, electric guitars and amps;
- materials to support classroom music-making such as published resources, home-grown resources, CD collections, etc.;
- materials to support extra-curricular music-making, e.g. sheet music;
- classroom-based teaching for one hour a week in Key Stage 3 and up to three hours a week in Key Stage 4;
- extra-curricular activities at lunchtime and after school;
- the chance to learn how to play a musical instrument for up to half an hour per week, usually with an instrumental teacher.

Task 1.8 The secondary school music department

1 When you were a pupil, how did your own school compare with the music department in Box 1.4?
2 How does the music department of your placement school(s) compare with Box 1.4?
3 Ask your mentor or school tutor to identify the features of a music department they would ideally like to work in.
4 Use this information as part of a 'compare and contrast' discussion with your peers.

---

can be up to half a day in length with up to 90 pupils involved and possibly five professionals. The theory is that such a set-up has the scope for flexibility, variety, creativity, exploiting interconnectedness of subjects, i.e. some of the ingredients of deep experience and learning.

What might a school music department look like and how might it be organised if we take the following things into consideration:

- a place where the individual interests of all pupils can be catered for;
- a place where there is genuine scope for pupil voice;
- a place where there is enough flexibility to make connections between other subjects and underpinning skills;
- a place where there is choice;
- a place where the individual learning needs of pupils can be taken into account;
- a place where the resources and support (human and physical) exist to make the first five points a reality?

On the back of such issues school managers and music teachers are asking fundamental questions about the purpose of music education; whether it needs to be a weekly timetabled subject; what physical resources are most appropriate and who should be the 'teachers'. It is the deep leadership of schools and music departments that will make deep experience, deep support and thus deep learning a reality. Task 1.9 is an opportunity for you to design a music department for the twenty-first century.

Task 1.9 Designing a music department for personalisation

Use Table 1.2 to draw or write about your ideas in each section; use your ideas to debate the shape of school music provision in the future. You might also take into consideration the approach to deep learning and deep experience noted elsewhere in this chapter, i.e. Musical Futures and the National Curriculum. Let no expense be spared! This is an opportunity to think out of the box; try not to get too bound up in the pragmatics at this stage.

Table 1.2 School music provision for the future

Physical design (the spaces)

Physical resources (i.e. the kit to play, compose, record and listen to music)

Human resources (who are the 'teachers' and what will they do?)

Supporting resources (published material of all types)

Access (when and how will pupils learn music, and will there be a timetable?)

SUMMARY

In this chapter we have seen how the nine gateways for personalisation have been reconfigured into four interconnected 'deeps'. The deeps and associated gateways help us to focus on the process of personalisation in music education. They offer a set of tools and strategies for enabling all pupils to engage and achieve in the music curriculum. The case studies are examples of how the deeps manifest themselves in music education and also show their interconnectedness. Deep learning can arise out of recognising the importance of pupils' informal experiences, which has significant implications for the types of deep experiences set up through the National Curriculum. Furthermore, informal pedagogy and learning presents issues of how and when to intervene in pupil learning (deep support) and how music departments should organise and timetable musical learning (deep leadership). Such connections present some exciting possibilities for music education in the twenty-first century.

FURTHER READING

Musical Futures: www.musicalfutures.org
This website contains many resources to support informal learning and pedagogy.

Music-ITE: www.music-ite.org.uk
This website contains a series of resources to provide further support for some of the main case studies found in this chapter, e.g. informal learning and pedagogy, the National Curriculum for Music.

Qualifications and Curriculum Authority: http://curriculum.qca.org.uk
Here can be found the details of the National Curriculum for Music and the justification for the underpinning aims and skills.

Teacher Net: www.teachernet.gov.uk
This website contains useful information in relation to all aspects of current government initiatives and where more resources can be found for BSF and talented musicians.

Chapter 2 Musical teaching and learning in 14–19 education

KEITH EVANS

INTRODUCTION

The number of pupils pursuing curriculum music beyond Key Stage 3 is relatively low. Figures released by the Qualifications and Curriculum Authority (QCA) in 2002 confirmed that the number of pupils taking GCSE music in each of the previous ten years had remained around 7 per cent (QCA 2002). The *2004/5 Annual Report on Curriculum and Assessment* for music was more encouraging in noting that 'in nearly 50 per cent of schools surveyed, the number of students opting for music in year 10 has increased' (QCA 2005: 18), but these statistics hardly reflect the importance given to music in young people's lives. In recent years there have been renewed efforts to ensure that courses and qualifications at KS4 and above are relevant and serve the needs of pupils. Successful teaching at this level has always emphasised practical musical engagement and been based on the full integration of musical skills. Recent changes have taken place in the context of the drive for personalisation, increased curriculum flexibility, and attempts to address the academic and vocational divide. These changes partly reflect demands to make qualifications and courses relevant, but large-scale reforms such as the universal offer of the new diploma have forced major reviews of the arts entitlement at 14–19.

OBJECTIVES

By the end of this chapter you should be able to:

- understand how to teach 14–19 courses musically;
- know the range of qualifications for 14–19 pupils and understand their different purposes and content;
- recognise the distinction between established qualifications and work-related pathways;
- plan different routes of progression in order to personalise the curriculum.

BUILDING ON KS3 AND TEACHING MUSICALLY

The importance of developing knowledge, skills and understanding through practical music-making and the integration of performing, composing and listening are key concepts in the revised KS3 National Curriculum (QCA 2007c), but they are fundamentals of good music teaching at any level. At KS4 these ideals are seemingly challenged by the assessment structures for qualifications such as GCSE and BTEC (the former Business and Technology Education Council awards), which divide skills such as performing and composing into separate papers or units. This does not mean that we abandon established good practice and start to structure the course with lessons focusing on discrete skills. The GCSE subject criteria for music (QCA 2007a), on which the revised specifications due to be introduced in September 2009 are based, reiterate that the three assessment objectives (performing, composing, and listening and appraising skills) are interrelated and the specifications actually reflect and reinforce this through requirements such as 'each piece (composition) will be based on a different Area of Study' (Edexcel 2008: 46) or the Integrated Tasks of the Oxford, Cambridge and RSA Examinations (OCR) specification where candidates are expected to compose for the instrument on which they perform.

There are many ways in which you can promote the integration of skills in your KS4 teaching. Box 2.1 gives some practical suggestions while developing ongoing skills.

Box 2.1 Integration of skills

Use whole-class performance to explore style and structure and as a starting point for composing

For example, as a class rehearse *I Got Rhythm* in order for pupils to gain 'knowledge of' 32-bar song form, or perform Terry Reilly's *In C* as a model for techniques of minimalism. Both of these are carried out prior to pupils working creatively in either style.

Link listening to performing and composing

For example, explore 'paired' works with a common musical process, e.g. the slow-moving bass ostinato in Pachelbel's *Canon* with *Samskeyti* by the Icelandic group Sigur Ros recorded in 2007. You could develop pupils' aural skills by asking them to join in with the repeating bass line. Exploring how the music unfolds in both pieces, they could then continue by aurally copying other parts and/or improvising and developing original melodic material over the established basses.

Use improvisation to develop confidence in performing and to explore creative processes

For example, on one occasion this might be building up ideas over a short chord sequence, on another the improvisation might be based around a series of riffs.

Consider the concept of rondo form. The idea of a recurring theme throughout a piece of music with contrasting 'breaks' is a straightforward one and a universal feature of music from Mozart to samba. You could simply *tell* the pupils the structure, for example, ABACADA, and believe they have the knowledge required for the examination. But such factual knowledge is limited without proper understanding, including the skill of applying the knowledge in different contexts. Moreover, the concept of rondo could be the starting point for a whole range of activities developing skills across performing, composing and listening. Examples are given in Box 2.2.

Box 2.2 Exploring rondo form

1 With the pupils in a circle, teach three or four short, distinctive eight-beat rhythms (drums or body percussion). Divide into groups and perform the different rhythms simultaneously. (This is the rondo theme.) After a set number of repetitions, one person improvises a break for an agreed number of beats before the rest of the group joins in again with the rondo theme. Do the same again, giving everyone an opportunity for an improvised solo within a recurring rondo structure.

Box 2.2 *continued*

2 Translate the activity above onto pitched instruments, setting pitch limitations, e.g. pentatonic ACDEG.
3 The activity is then developed using a harmonic framework.
  (a) Introduce a chord sequence as the basis for a new rondo theme
    e.g. Am / Dm / G / C / F / Bdim / Em / Am /
    Students adapt this to their instrument (e.g. guitars / keyboards play chords; bass instruments play riffs; voices / melodic instruments perform simple improvised melodies).
  (b) Individual pupils create improvised solo episodes in contrasting tonalities (C major, Dorian on D) while a simple two-chord backing sequence is played by the rest of the group
    e.g. C / G / C / G / C / G / C - G / C /
    or Dm / Am / Dm / Am / Dm / Am / Dm - Am / Dm /
  (c) Returning to the chord sequence in stage 3(a), pupils work collectively to compose a main rondo theme for the instruments available. They improvise and later 'fix' their own (unaccompanied) episodes in between with the specific brief of exploiting the characteristics of their instrument.

Note how the students experience and get to know rondo form through these activities. They develop performing (solo and ensemble), improvising and listening skills in the process, and activity 3(c) leads naturally into an individual composing task, if required. Short, related listening tasks could be interspersed and, as a whole, these activities are the basis for a unit of work. There is a further example of integration in practice in Box 5.5 of *Learning to Teach Music in the Secondary School* (Philpott and Spruce 2007).

Integration of the full range of musical skills will not be possible in all lessons and there may be the odd occasion when it is not even desirable, but there is no doubt that learning will be more musical and ultimately more effective if this is adopted as a basic principle. Now carry out Task 2.1.

Task 2.1 Integrated teaching at KS4

Think back to a KS4 lesson you have taught, observed or been taught where there was a single focus on either performing, composing or listening. Decide how the lesson could have been changed to incorporate a range of musical skills. Use the grid below to show how this move to a more integrated approach might look in practice.

Learning objectives		
Original single focus	Possible opportunities for: Performing Composing Listening	Possible integration of performing, composing and listening

TEACHING AS OR A LEVEL GCE MUSICALLY

The 2008 revisions to A level GCE introduced a four-unit structure for most subjects but Music continues to maintain a six-unit A level with three 'units' in both AS and A2 corresponding essentially to performing, composing and listening/analysing. Nevertheless, awarding bodies still make encouraging statements about how the specification extends 'the GCSE skills of Performing, Composing and Appraising *'in ways which emphasise their interdependence'* (OCR 2008: 4) or how the areas of study *'provide opportunities not only for the study of repertoire but also for the development of musical ideas through composing and performing activities'* (Edexcel 2007: 17). These statements emphasise that teachers must seek to overcome artificial barriers and make meaningful links.

In teaching any AS or A level course in music you need to prepare pupils for a range of tasks within the three key areas of musical activity. At different stages pupils are expected to show competence in

- performing (solo and with others)
- composing original pieces of music
- compositional techniques exercises
- aural perception – dictation, chord recognition, etc.
- aural awareness of different styles
- analysis (aurally and by reference to a score)
- understanding music history and continuity and change over time.

Once again, because these skills are assessed separately does not mean that they have to be taught as separate entities. Taken *together*, they are the means through which pupils develop and demonstrate their musical understanding. The example in Box 2.3 shows how you might introduce a set work practically, at the same time developing aural awareness, performing skills and creativity.

Box 2.3 A practical introduction to Schubert: *Der Doppelganger* (an Edexcel A level set work)

The pupils would work through this series of tasks *prior* to hearing or seeing the score.

1 Play the chord sequence very slowly a number of times and invite pupils to listen carefully and join in at a suitable pitch on their instruments. Continue to repeat until everyone is playing. Discuss the mood (sombre, sinister – why?)

2 Reveal the notation and play again.
3 Invite individual pupils to take turns improvising on one note (F#) while others continue with chords.
4 Pupils again take turns to improvise. This time they improvise melodies (no longer restricted to F#) to fit the lyrics below.

The night is still,   The streets are calm,   In this near-by house   lived my love.

Box 2.3 *continued*

5 Introduce the expressive potential of the appoggiatura and, with subsequent improvisations, encourage pupils to introduce a 'leaning note' into the final note of each phrase. For example:

6 Introduce the two alternatives below for the chord in bar 8. Consider their effect in performance. Continue to perform, as above, but experiment with all three possibilities for bar 8 in turn.

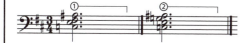

7 Devise a group improvisation or composition based on the material explored so far.

Through taking part in such activities pupils become familiar with the raw materials of the work – in this case, the bare repeating chords, the short hesitant phrases, the expressive use of dissonance and some extraordinary chromatic harmony. When they then go on to hear the Schubert it is with a heightened awareness of the compositional processes. Now carry out Task 2.2.

Task 2.2 A creative approach to set works

Choose a work or an extract from a work that is the focus for A level study. Identify the key musical features and devise a series of practical activities similar to the ones in Box 2.3 as an introduction to exploring the work with pupils. In planning, it is worth considering:

- the importance of pupils performing with instruments or voices
- the potential of aural learning
- the role of improvisation
- how you might stimulate composing.

ALTERNATIVE PATHWAYS

The traditional pattern of GCSE followed by A level as the standard qualification route in music has been challenged for some time. By the early years of the twenty-first century a significant number of schools have abandoned GCSE Music in favour of a range of qualifications such as the BTEC First Certificate and Diploma, National Council for Further Education (NCFE) courses in music technology. In many schools, music has not been a discrete subject in the curriculum at KS4, but has been included as one discipline within a collaborative arts course such as GCSE Expressive Arts or BTEC Performing Arts. There is similar diversity post 16 with BTEC Nationals, the International Baccalaureate and an A level in Music Technology all challenging the traditional Music A level. From September 2008 the introduction of the Diploma in Creative and Media at both KS4 and post 16 offers further choice.

This diversity has come about for a number of reasons including:

- schools wishing to offer courses which are more attractive to their students;
- schools having the flexibility to promote a range of qualifications of similar standing as a result of the introduction of the National Qualifications Framework (NQF);
- schools wishing to move away from formal examinations;
- schools wishing to personalise the curriculum.

It is therefore important that you take time to investigate some of the alternatives and consider the relative merits of equivalent qualifications.

The NQF was devised by the QCA to accredit and establish parity between qualifications on the basis of a scale of eight levels. The positioning of qualifications at the same level indicates that they are broadly comparable in terms of general level and outcome. (See Table 6.4 in *Learning to Teach Music in the Secondary School*.)

The linked National Database of Accredited Qualifications (www.accreditedqualifications. org.uk/index.aspx) includes numerous qualifications available at level 2 (equivalent to GCSE grades A*–C) which could be considered as possible alternatives to GCSE and significant numbers at level 3 (equivalent to A level). Alternatives to GCSE Music at level 2 currently include the following:

- Edexcel BTEC First Certificate/First Diploma in Music (www.edexcel.org.uk);
- NCFE Level 2 Certificate in Music Technology (www.ncfe.org.uk);
- Rock School Level 2 Diploma for Music Practitioners (www.rockschool.co.uk in conjunction with Access to Music www.accesstomusic.co.uk);
- Music as a component in the Assessment and Qualifications Alliance (AQA) GCSE Expressive Arts (www.aqa.org.uk);
- Music as a component in the AQA Applied GCSE Performing Arts (www.aqa.org.uk).

Task 2.3 involves researching alternatives to GCSE Music.

Task 2.3 Researching alternatives to GCSE: 1

With your colleagues, share research into two or three of the alternative level 2 qualifications. For each qualification, find out and compare information such as

- the main aims and focus of the qualification;
- the balance between performing, composing, arranging and listening;
- the balance between making music and gaining knowledge *about* music and the music industry;
- the potential for using music technology;
- the balance between coursework and formal examinations;
- its equivalence (e.g. BTEC First Certificate is 'worth' the equivalent of two GCSEs A*–C);
- the links with other subjects.

Flexibility is a particular strength of the BTEC qualifications. The BTEC First Certificate, for example, comprises the compulsory unit Planning and Creating a Music Product plus two further units from a choice of more than a dozen possibilities. Teachers are encouraged to write their own assignments and, given the variety of choice in the specialist units, there is genuine scope to tailor the course to the interests and strengths of the pupils. Figure 2.1 shows three possible combinations of units, and Task 2.4 follows on from this.

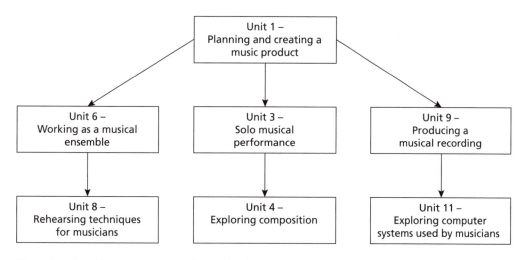

Figure 2.1 Possible combinations of units for the BTEC First Certificate in Music

---

Task 2.4 Researching alternatives to GCSE: 2

1 Consider whether any of the suggested course combinations in Figure 2.1 cater for the musical interests of KS4 pupils in the school where you are working.
2 What would be the implications of adopting any of the alternatives you explored in Task 2.3? Consider areas such as the profile of pupils, resources and accommodation, teacher expertise, timetabling and so on.

There is a clear work-related focus to BTEC qualifications with the intention that pupils learn and are assessed through assignments linked to realistic work-based scenarios. Similar 'applied learning' principles also underpin the diploma in Creative and Media, where at least half of the principal learning is expected to be set in a work-related context. Although the ideas for good 14–19 music teaching covered already in this chapter apply equally to such courses, there are features of the content, assessment structure and underlying principles of these courses which have important implications for how you teach. For example, the Learning Outcomes for most units focus on planning, implementation and evaluation; therefore, although the resulting product could be judged from a technical or artistic point of view, assessment is largely based on the preparation and process. A typical unit Rehearsal Techniques for Musicians from the BTEC First Certificate has the following stated learning outcomes:

1 Know how to prepare a detailed rehearsal schedule.
2 Know how to set challenging and achievable targets for a rehearsal session.
3 Understand how to evaluate progress critically.
4 Be able to demonstrate technical and musical control of an instrument within a group.

The focus here is clearly on the *process* of rehearsing with relatively little emphasis on the *outcome*. From the pupils' point of view the unit is concerned with self-awareness, analysing progress and setting targets. As their teacher, your role for much of the time is to offer advice, provide support and generally oversee progress. This is not to say you have nothing to teach. There is plenty to be explored, for example, in terms of what and how to rehearse and about different rehearsal practices in the industry. Picking up on general principles from earlier in this chapter, a well-run rehearsal at the start of the unit with a group of pupils led by the teacher could offer plenty of opportunities for critical analysis.

The link between the assignments you set and the quality of evidence the pupils present is crucial in BTEC and diploma courses. An assignment is typically framed as a series of tasks that guide the pupils through the investigation – planning – production – evaluation cycle. While there are an increasing number of published resources to give ideas, such as Julia Winterson (2002) *50 Music Assignments for the BTEC First Diploma*, your pupils will benefit if you can personalise the course to their needs. They also need careful guidance on the most suitable evidence for assessment purposes. Traditional written evidence is an obvious starting point, but recordings of interviews, presentations, video evidence, blogs, etc. might be more engaging. Now carry out Task 2.5.

Task 2.5 Planning for work-related learning

1 Draw up an original assignment to address the learning objectives in the unit *Rehearsal Techniques for Musicians* (above) or any other unit from a BTEC or Creative and Media diploma course. This will involve a series of smaller tasks which correspond to the investigation to evaluation stages suggested earlier.
2 Identify *four* different assessment points at which the pupils could evidence their learning. Only *one* of these should involve a written task.

You may wish to refer to tutor support materials for the BTEC qualification at www.edexcel.org.uk and other online support for diplomas from all awarding bodies.

PROGRESSION

The reforms to A level Music in 2000 were seen as the finishing touch in bringing about a seamless progression from KS3 to post 16 study and, for the first time, the integration of musical skills established by the National Curriculum was promoted throughout the 14–19 phase. Pupils who enjoy and achieve in music during KS3 are now better placed to choose the subject as one of their options at KS4 and, if they wish, continue their study at a higher level beyond the age of 16. Compared with the mid- to late 1990s, option groups for music in most schools comprise a much broader spread of musical abilities and interests. In some schools, innovative teaching at KS3 (e.g. the Musical Futures informal learning model) and an increasing recognition of pupils' experience beyond the classroom has started to address the poor take-up for music as an examination subject. However, as well as enthusing your pupils to continue your subject, you have a responsibility to ensure they make informed choices based on a detailed understanding of what is involved in the study of music at the next stage.

The popularity of Musical Futures in year 9 has had a significant impact on the number of pupils pursuing their studies into KS4 – an average 24 per cent take-up in the first two years in the Hertfordshire pathfinder schools, compared with a less than 10 per cent national average (Price 2007: 16). It is clear, however, that unless the courses and teaching at KS4 can be adapted to include informal learning practices, these 'new' pupils will be frustrated and their expectations unfulfilled. A solution could lie in the choice of qualification and some teachers have concluded that BTEC and less traditional courses are the obvious route of progression. However, an alternative approach might be to reflect on how you are currently teaching the GCSE course and see how informal learning practices might be adopted here. Read the case study in Box 2.4 and note how these GCSE pupils are drawing on their own (varied) musical backgrounds, working collaboratively, learning by copying, developing instrumental technique, and constantly making music. Then carry out Task 2.6.

Box 2.4   GCSE lesson case study

A controlled-assessment (coursework) task requires the pupils to compose a piece in variation form. The class includes Pupil A (a violinist and guitarist), Pupil B (a self-taught rock guitarist) and Pupil C (a jazz pianist who largely plays by ear).

Pupil A feels he knows about variations, having played a set of decorative variations for his recent Grade 5 violin exam. Consequently, he has taken a very simple melody from an earlier tutor book and composed a couple of variations by adding scales and ornaments to the theme. In discussion with his teacher, he decides that his composition would benefit from some accompaniment, and has therefore asked Player C to add a few supporting chords on the piano while he plays the theme. As they play together the pianist adds a few bluesy touches and they go on to explore some ideas for a jazz variation.

Pupil B has decided to base her variations on a repeating chord sequence so she strums through some familiar riffs before settling on an original eight-chord pattern. Her intention is that the piece will gradually build from gentle beginnings to a frantic rock climax. She wants to work on some of the later lead guitar solos so she enlists the help of Pupil A (who plays in her band) on guitar to keep the supporting chords going while the teacher adds some rhythm on the drums. Player A constantly stumbles in changing between two chords but this is easily rectified when Player B shows him a simpler fingering.

Task 2.6   Informal learning and GCSE

What are the conditions and assumptions that have led to the lesson described in Box 2.4? Draw out the distinctive features of this lesson by making notes in the table below. Consider the extent to which these features are reflected in your current practice or the practice you have observed in GCSE lessons in school.

Feature	Notes
Classroom conditions	
Task set	
Role of the teacher	
Working relationships	
Other	

As we have seen already, there is a wide variety of qualifications to choose from for further study in music. Progression is now much more complex than the traditional KS3 – GCSE – A level route. Given the distinct nature and purpose of different qualifications, the possibility of a personalised pathway linked to the interests and strengths of the individual is a reality (although this may involve attending courses at neighbouring institutions).

SUMMARY

In this chapter we have seen that successful music teaching in the 14–19 phase is based on the seamless integration of performing, composing and listening and is firmly rooted in practical musical experience. It is by performing that pupils appreciate the effect of music and gain first-hand knowledge of musical processes. Good teachers focus pupil attention on the *sound* of music, and aural copying and 'real-time' composing (improvisation) play an important part here.

There is an increasing range of competing qualifications at this level with work-related courses challenging established GCSE and A levels. Schools can tailor provision to pupils' musical interests, and collaboration *between* schools could go some way to fulfilling the promise of a more personalised curriculum. New pedagogies need to be implemented across the 14–19 phase to capitalise on the success of informal learning practices.

FURTHER READING

Bray, D. (2000) 'Effective GCSE teaching' and 'Effective teaching of post-16 examination courses', in *Teaching Music in the Secondary School*. Oxford: Oxford University Press. These chapters will help you understand the importance of translating the basic requirements of a published examination specification into worthwhile musical experiences.

Bray, D. (2000) 'An examination of GCSE music uptake rates', *British Journal of Music Education*, 17(1): 79–89. An interesting exploration of examination entries in the early years of GCSE which suggested that the qualification was not proving to be as successful or attractive to students as intended.

Evans, K. (2006) 'AS/A2: an integrated approach to teaching set works', *Classroom Music*, 3(2): 45–48. A practical approach to the study of A level set works is suggested and exemplified through a series of improvised activities linked to a Shostakovich Prelude and Fugue.

Wright, R. (2002) 'Music for all? Pupils' perceptions of the GCSE Music examination in one South Wales secondary school', *British Journal of Music Education*, 19(3): 227–241. Further research which highlights the problem of making GCSE Music accessible to all in the light of the perceived advantage for pupils having additional instrumental or vocal tuition outside the classroom.

Department for Children, Schools and Families: www.dcsf.gov.uk/14–19
The DCSF website for 14–19 education and skills gives a good overview of the latest 14–19 reforms.

Part 2 Developing musical pedagogy

Chapter 3   Cultural understanding

JOHN FINNEY

INTRODUCTION: WHAT IS CULTURAL UNDERSTANDING?

It is important to value music as a set of processes, skills and formal elements that give the subject structure and distinction. However, for music to claim a place in the school and to become a part of a general education, it needs to look outward and reveal its social and cultural significance. We are interested in why people make music, how they do it and what makes their way of doing it in some way unique and important to them. In turn, such interest informs what we do and why we do it. What emerges from this process is cultural understanding.

OBJECTIVES

By the end of this chapter you should be able to:

- understand what is meant by 'cultural understanding';
- plan for teaching cultural understanding;
- know how cultural understanding is gained through practical engagement with a work of art;
- consider ways of avoiding pupil alienation when introducing unfamiliar music;
- understand the fluidity of postmodern culture and musical identity.

CULTURE IS ORDINARY

'Culture' is one of the two or three most difficult words in the English language. In response, Raymond Williams (1980) maintains that culture is best thought of as 'ordinary'. In this way, we avoid paying too much attention to cultural objects, pieces of music detached from time and place. We avoid reducing music to a set of conventions without regard for the social conditions in which the music was created and recreated. Williams also writes about the 'selective tradition'. This is the process over time whereby some work is preserved, given special attention, and some not. The idea that what survives does so because of the 'test of time' is a silly abstraction. 'Time' by itself can't do anything. It is people and groups of people who make selections to create patterns of culture. And so we might ask why it is that the eighteenth-century tradition of 'Rough Music' (see Thompson 1993), music made in rural communities of England using whatever was at hand to 'drum out' those that were unwelcome (and more recently manifest in the playing of recorded classical music in public places intended to 'drum out' loitering youth), is much less likely to be found in programmes of study than Bach Chorale. Thinking about this process of selection will lead to healthy dispute about what to teach and why to teach it, and whose music and musical practices are considered educationally worthwhile.

DIFFERENCE AND DIVERSITY

Thinking of culture as 'ordinary' leads to a consideration of difference and diversity and interest in particular people in particular places at particular times and circumstances. It becomes of interest that J.S. Bach incorporated the chorale into his religious musical dramas. Why did he do this? What would a Lutheran church service have sounded like at the time of Bach; what does it sound like now? The challenge is always to move from generalisations and potential ignorance towards the particularities of lived experience. It would be unthinkable to teach Bach Chorale without context.

Why teach the Blues?

How might we approach the Blues, a form of music that embraces a vast range of musical practices living in widely differing contexts? We can identify formal elements thought to be common to all cases of Blues: a particular chord sequence, certain melodic characteristics and so on. But is this what is important about the Blues? Is it this that is important to those who made it, make it now? Why *are* we teaching the Blues? See Task 3.1.

Task 3.1 Why teach the Blues?

Below are nine possible reasons for teaching the Blues. Write each out on a slip of paper and create a diamond nine. A diamond nine is a strategy for working out beliefs and values. At the top of the diamond is placed that which is of paramount importance, the one thing that must be. Below the two next, then three, then two and finally the least significant. A good move is to reject one altogether and to create a fresh one. Working with another person or in a group on this task will lead to debate and the clarification of values.

- a harmonic progression can be introduced;
- improvisation skill can be developed;
- *Hanging in the Breeze* can be listened to, the music signalling everybody to stand at the end of the evening at the New York Blues Club;
- a Blues 'feel' can be had;
- the school's most experienced Blues musician can lead the work;
- students can learn about blue notes;
- students can feel the Blues through their voice;
- it is useful preparation for writing cadences;
- a song can be written about the people trafficking, read about in the local newspaper.

Create similar lists relating to other genres of music. This method will serve well as a first stage in planning a sequence of work.

Consider:
1 What will be of interest to the pupils, both locally and globally?
2 What will support learning the structure of music?

Task 3.1 *continued*

3 What local resources (within the school community and beyond) can be called upon?
4 What musical skills and cultural specific techniques will be needed?
5 How will a physical empathy – feel for the music – be gained?
6 What will challenge preconceptions and lead to critical thinking and debate?
7 How will the topic need to be approached in order to make sense for differing ages and ways of being interested?

Ask your pupils to discuss why the Blues should be learnt. What priorities will *they* suggest? How would they plan a sequence of learning? What is of most importance to them?

FINDING CULTURAL DEPTH

Coming to know a work of art and something of why it was made, how it came into being and why it is important to those who continue to perform it, can help to contextualise our own practical engagement with it. How might this be done? In Box 3.1 we see pupils taken on a journey of discovery that develops empathic understanding with a time and place. They are learning to be composers and coming to appreciate the creative process of another composer.

Box 3.1 Scenario 1

Eighteen girls aged 11–16 are gathered in the large rehearsal room in their school's music department. With double basses in one corner and orchestral percussion in another, they have come to take part in a project that will take them out of school, beyond their immediate city environs to the Barbican Concert Hall in London, where they will hear the Fifth Symphony of Gustav Mahler in two days' time. They have in common a commitment to playing an orchestral instrument and this they bring with them to the beginning of the day where they meet animateur Hannah, who will lead them during the day and in their pre-concert performance at the Barbican in two days' time.

They form a circle and, following introductions, Hannah creates a movement – sound sequence figuratively faithful to motives from the symphony's first movement, the 'Trauermarsch'. The musical material transmitted is Mahler's. There are 15 minutes of intensive working where Hannah gives and the girls give back, where Hannah insists through repetition that all get it. They get melodic fragments as well as rhythmic ones. 'You really need to get hold of this material, this is very important'. Hannah reveals Mahler's use of the song 'Der Tambourg'sell', a song about one of Mahler's ill-fated 'children', a drummer boy condemned to execution and his long walk to death, the 'Trauermarsch'. The girls want to know what it is that the boy has done that deserves such a fate. However, this is to remain a mystery for the time being. The work proceeds until groups have created their own 'Trauermarschen'.

In the minds of the girls live the drummer boy and his fate and the musical ideas and feelings that are now theirs as well as Mahler's.

In Scenario 1, the students' work is linked to a time and a place in at least four ways. There is the time and place of the drummer's execution, the moment of Mahler's response to it, the music room here and now as a time of being together and being part of a cultural event, and finally the experience of performing at the Barbican and being a part of an audience. Of interest too are the possibilities opened up for development of work across the curriculum and particularly the other arts. We might imagine other media such as writing, poetry, film, video, art work and movement-dance supporting and giving even greater depth and meaning to the work. And there may have been further out-of-school learning opportunities opened up. Task 3.2 shows how you could begin to develop cultural understanding through a practical in-depth engagement with a musical work.

Task 3.2 Finding cultural depth

Select a piece of music that you find inspiring. Take the following steps:

1 Identify the music's most distinctive features through playing or singing along to a recording. These might be melodic motives, rhythmic fragments, a story line, a rhythmic groove, the portrayal of a character, a riff, etc.
2 In a group use some of these as a starting point to create a new piece.
3 Make a recording and compare with the original.
4 Now go beyond emulation; develop and extend ideas.
5 Refine and make a further recording.
6 Offer this to a new group to emulate and develop.
7 Present the original piece for discussion.
8 Discuss how this kind of process could be used in school.
9 Discuss how this process could facilitate the development of cultural depth.

CULTURAL UNDERSTANDING AND IDENTITY

Paul Willis (1990) asks, 'How are the young already culturally energised?' This reminds us that young people come to school, come to any music educational setting, already with a culture of their own and knowing how to learn. They will have already explored a range of musical identities, reflected upon these and be ready to meet new cultural experiences with critical minds. So what will year 9 make of Klezmer and what will trainee teacher Alison make of teaching it? In Box 3.2, Scenario 2 is an account of this case study.

Box 3.2 Scenario 2

Alison had become a member of a Klezmer band in the first term of her training year. Two of the band had studied Klezmer as part of their first degree and quickly enthused Alison and others in the group. While Klezmer was new to Alison, her experience of folk-fiddle helped her to get inside the music. In researching Klezmer, Alison learnt about its turbulent history and how the music had come to be recognised as a distinctive genre at the beginning of the twentieth century and often referred to as 'Yiddish' music. Alison learnt about its role at weddings and as a form of entertainment. It was intriguing too that singer Amy Winehouse had incorporated Klezmer elements into her music.

Alison's first lesson exposed students to a variety of Klezmer music. The dancing of the Hora with very specific hand-clapping techniques to accompany was a high spot; boys

---

Box 3.2 *continued*

in one circle, girls in another. (Alison's Klezmer band had performed at a Jewish Society function and she had noted separate male–female segregated dancing.) Improvisation with Klezmer modes and characteristic rapid keyboard vamping and the quickening of tempo followed. Most successful of all proved to be a whole lesson devoted to singing, working as a whole class to refine performance and to get inside the character of Yiddish vocalisation. What Alison found most interesting was the realisation by her classes that this musical experience represented another way of life, and that for some of her students this may have been a little intimidating. 'Why would people dance to sad music at weddings and why male–female segregated dancing'? were the kinds of questions raised by students and that made the point well about the culture's 'difference' and strangeness.

In smaller group work that followed there were different levels of response. Some wholeheartedly entered into this new cultural experience and found an appropriate celebratory mood, others were more circumspect and their work lacked commitment. This has led Alison to rethink how such work might best be approached in the future. Clearly, meeting the unknown can be a challenge for students and may lead to cultural dissonance and to a feeling of alienation.

Lucy Green (2002) has shown how, when we experience music, two kinds of meaning are invoked. One arises from the meanings 'delineated' by what is experienced. Associations are rapidly made with what is heard and these may be positive or negative. The other form of meaning comes from the inner workings of the music itself, the meaning is 'inherent'. In Alison's teaching 'inherent' meaning had the potential to develop once her students were inside the music through their dance and song and if commitment can be gained here then it may be easier to move towards positive delineations and an interest in what might otherwise be strange. Task 3.3 provides an approach to test out where students are encouraged to be inquisitive about what is a new experience.

Task 3.3 Managing unfamiliar music in the classroom

1 How might Alison respond to her experiences with Klezmer in the classroom? What would be the impact on her planning next time?
2 After introducing music that is unfamiliar to pupils through the use of authentic performance activity, ask them in pairs to write down what they want to know about, why the music is like it is, and why it is performed in this way. For example, working as a samba band students might ask: can anybody be a leader? Working as a class minimalist ensemble: does the music ever change?

LIQUID CULTURE

According to Zygmunt Bauman (2000) we live in the age of Liquid Modernity where nothing is fixed or stable. Everything is fluid, changing and temporary. This may be another useful way of thinking about culture and cultural understanding. Bauman believes it is ever more difficult to establish stable identity. In the case of music this leads to developing multiple musical identities and coming to see music as without boundaries defined by genre and tradition and being in an endlessly fluid state of becoming something different. This is what postmodern culture proclaims. It is no longer possible to create new styles of expression, rather instead to see the past endlessly reused and for pastiche, the imitation of a peculiar or unique style becomes the most obvious means of expression (see Frederick Jameson 1998). Amy Winehouse's use of Klezmer elements is an example and this is not simply a matter of fusion. If fusion is the combining of two or more musical genres then here we are meaning something different and thinking in terms of pastiche and music as kaleidoscopic. The students who were introduced to Klezmer music will be expert at the appropriation of cultural material and this means making of it what is useful to them. It will be available to be reused. Music travels well.

For example, Julien Jacob, so we are told from reading his website, moved from Benin in West Africa to France in early childhood. While meeting a new culture he claims the imprint of African chant and rhythms from his native country. He tells of diverse influences such as Jazz, traditional African, mystical oriental chants as well as 1970s pop-rock. The track *Kalicom* is an example of his invention of a mysterious language. Now carry out Task 3.4.

Task 3.4 Exploring liquid culture

1 Make use of the internet to find examples of contemporary artists and their music and investigate the range of influences that have played a part in the making of their musical identities. Make a list of these influences and examples of how they are evident in the music. This is how it works in *Kalicom*.

Influences	Examples
Jazz	Rhythmic drive
Mystical oriental chant	Vocalisations
1970s rock	Simple chord accompaniment
Traditional African	Drumming cross-rhythms

2 Plan for 'kaleidoscopic' music-making with students through research tasks relating to their preferred artists and what has influenced them. Working through the medium of music technology may be most appropriate.

WHAT SHALL WE TEACH AND HOW SHALL WE TEACH IT?

The statement 'what music is taught is only slightly more important than the way it is taught' is offered from time to time as a challenge to music teachers. But perhaps the way music is taught might be influenced, if not determined, by what is taught and for what purpose and with what context in mind. In this way it might be possible to bring stronger ethos and greater depth to a musical workshop and to make more worthwhile musical events: Klezmer music taught through characteristic movement and shared with the local Jewish community; traditional shanties taught through movement and leading to a Shanty Festival; Senegalese Drumming learnt in a circle with leadership distributed in spontaneous fashion; Steve Reich's *Different Trains* and its underlying narrative linked to the Holocaust and the theme of 'separation'; Bach Chorale taught through vocal performance; the making of Rough Music with electronic sounds and designed for a particular place; recreating a Victorian Music Hall drawing upon the diverse talents of the group including out-of-school talents; making the classroom the site for a courtroom rap opera concerned with the workings of the criminal justice system; global internet musical improvisation; ideas of democracy in the compositional techniques of John Cage; bringing groups together to sing in many different languages and so on. These are examples of richer contexts and richer forms of learning that will lead to deeper cultural understanding.

The challenge for the music teacher is to be resourceful and to remain culturally alive, to search out new ways of being musical and to continually ask why music is being made, why it is so important to those who make it and in what ways it is related to a way of life that might be similar or very different to their own and their students'. The National Curriculum 2007 *aims* for all young people to become successful learners who enjoy learning, make progress and achieve and become confident individuals who contribute to society. The development of cultural understanding through music will play a part in this. Culture is something to talk about, to argue about and while our classrooms and other places will be sounding out culture through the music being created, there is a time and place for a culture debate, a time for talking about it, for arguing and contesting ideas about the beliefs and values of each other close by and far away. Task 3.5 illustrates how to set up a culture debate.

Task 3.5 Setting up a culture debate

Here are some possible topics for debate:
- Music divides people as much as it unites them.
- What is taught is more important than how it is taught.
- A culture can be fully understood only by those who are part of it.

A culture debate for student teachers and their pupils could follow these steps:
1 Decide on the issue to be discussed.
2 Ask each member of the class to write down a thought, question or idea in response.
3 These are elicited in turn and written on the board; each contributor is thanked by name.
4 The group vote on which is to be the starting point for the group discussion.
5 The discussion begins with the idea selected being explained further by its author.
6 The discussion proceeds.
7 The group may need to decide on ground rules or these may evolve naturally.
8 The teacher takes no part.
9 The group cease deferring to the teacher and gain autonomy.
10 Has the group talked itself into better cultural understanding?

SUMMARY

Recognising that 'culture' is one of the most difficult words in the English language, this chapter has introduced you to ways of thinking about it in the context of teaching music. It has set out to do this through activities that 'integrate practice', nurture 'critical understanding', 'creativity' and 'communication'. 'Cultural understanding' is central to the National Curriculum's 'key concepts'.

A major theme running through the chapter has been to think of culture as being about people and their differences. This gives to the music teacher the role of exploring with students the ways in which music is not only a matter of processes, skills and formal elements, but also about beliefs and values and ways of life that make up musical identities. In this way music in school can be of great personal and social significance to those who are educated through it, helping them to see culture as both ordinary and extra-ordinary.

FURTHER READING

Thompson, E.P. (1993) *Customs in Common: Studies in Traditional Popular Culture.* New York: The New Press.

Williams, R. (1980) *The Long Revolution.* London: Penguin.

There are relatively few writings or resources which deal explicitly with the pedagogy of cultural understanding but these two books are an excellent primer to issues surrounding the nature of culture.

Chapter 4   Teaching and learning for critical thinking and understanding

GARY SPRUCE

INTRODUCTION

Although the National Curriculum (QCA 2007c) is now in its fourth version, critical thinking and critical understanding are identified for the first time as something which should be addressed in and through young people's education. Critical thinking is linked in the generic National Curriculum documentation with creative thinking. However, whereas extensive guidance is given in the general curriculum documentation as to how creativity might be recognised and promoted, critical thinking is explicitly referred to in part of just one sentence as involving 'evaluative reasoning'.

The National Curriculum programme of study for music at Key Stage 3 identifies 'critical understanding' as one of the key concepts which 'underpin the study of music' and suggests that critical understanding should be developed through:

- Engaging with and analysing music, developing views and justifying opinions.
- Drawing on experience of a wide range of musical styles and contexts to inform judgements.

(QCA 2007c: 180)

While evaluative reasoning is an important aspect of critical thinking, and developing views and opinions based upon experience of a wide range of musical styles and contexts provide an important arena within which critical thinking and development of critical understanding can take place, what is absent from the National Curriculum is any explicit definition of what critical thinking and understanding are in either a general or musical sense. Neither is any guidance given as to the necessary preconditions or pedagogy which might enable critical thinking and understanding to take place.

This chapter will argue that, properly embedded, critical thinking and understanding enable pupils to make connections between their musical learning in school and their lived reality. In order to enable pupils to develop critical thinking and understanding this chapter will argue that teachers have to examine commonly held assumptions about the relationship between 'knowledge' and 'the learner' and how 'knowledge', 'truth' and 'understanding' is formed (constructed) by the learner. Critical thinking and understanding consequently presents a significant challenge to many conventional pedagogical models of teaching and learning. However, the rewards of critical thinking and understanding in music are a music education which empowers pupils.

OBJECTIVES

By the end of this chapter you should be able to:

- understand what critical thinking and understanding are and their implications for music teaching and learning;
- understand the relationship between knowledge, the learner and critical thinking and understanding;
- understand how critical thinking skills can support musical learning and understanding;
- devise teaching and learning strategies to support the development of critical thinking and understanding within the music curriculum.

WHAT IS CRITICAL THINKING AND UNDERSTANDING?

Although definitions abound it is generally agreed that critical thinking and understanding involve:

- a conscious process of gathering, analysing, synthesising and evaluating information in order to act upon it;
- the ability to question assumptions and 'self-evident' truths;
- a willingness to reflect upon and justify one's own beliefs and opinions and adopt an open-minded approach to those of others;
- the ability to construct coherent and well-reasoned arguments and to be able to communicate these to others;
- a willingness to adopt a systematic approach to problem solving.

Now carry out Task 4.1.

Task 4.1 Critical thinking and understanding

Construct a table similar to Table 4.1 and, in discussion with other student teachers, identify:

- examples from your own learning where you have drawn on or developed your critical thinking and understanding;
- examples from your own teaching, or teaching that you have observed (in any subject), that has allowed pupils to demonstrate these critical thinking skills.

It is likely that both your own experiences and your observations of children were positive, for the characteristics of critical thinking and understanding outlined above are also characteristics of an 'empowered learner': one who has ownership of *what* and *how* they learn. An 'empowered learner' is generally a happy and willing learner. Without this empowerment – this ownership of learning – it is difficult to conceive of how critical thinking and understanding can be developed or demonstrated.

Table 4.1 Auditing critical thinking and understanding

Critical thinking and understanding	Examples from your own learning	Examples of pupils' learning
Evaluating information in order to act upon it		
Questioning assumptions		
Reflecting upon and justifying opinions		
Constructing coherent and well-reasoned arguments		
Adopting a systematic approach to learning		

Task 4.2 Critical thinking, understanding and music education

As you work through this chapter you will explore, through its text and activities, different aspects of critical thinking and understanding (including those identified above within musical contexts), i.e. you will consider what critical thinking and understanding mean for music teaching and learning. Either using a table similar to the one constructed for Task 4.1, or some other form of record, first note down your present thoughts about how critical thinking skills and understanding might be developed through music teaching and learning. Add to these thoughts as you proceed through the chapter. You will be asked to return to this activity at the end of the chapter.

CREATING THE CONDITIONS FOR CRITICAL THINKING AND UNDERSTANDING

In this section we are going to consider the conditions that need to be in place to enable children to develop and demonstrate critical thinking and understanding.

Musical knowledge and the learner

A common-sense view of knowledge perceives it as being something which is 'fixed' (unchanged by context or use), is 'out there' waiting to be learnt and is something which the learner plays no part in defining, constructing or (least of all) changing. It is the knowledge equivalent of the supermarket pre-cooked meal.

Such knowledge is sometimes described as 'objective' or 'propositional' knowledge. Examples might include knowing the instruments of the orchestra, the number of strings on a violin or what a riff is. Such knowledge might also include knowing how to recognise an ostinato, or play a scale or clap a particular rhythm.

In *Learning to Teach Music in the Secondary School*, Philpott (2007a: 29–30) defines such knowledge as:

- knowledge 'about' music: the 'facts' of music such as knowing the instruments in a string quartet;
- knowledge of 'how' music, such as how to clap a crotchet–quaver–quaver rhythm.

Although such knowledge is not without value as a means of informing musical learning and experience, it is problematic in a number of respects, particularly if it is the only kind of music knowledge children come into contact with in school. Because it is fixed, the learner has no personal investment in it and consequently the 'knowledge' often does not reflect or add to the pupils' understanding of 'their' world. Children therefore do not buy into it.

Second, such knowledge is abstracted from real musical contexts. Knowing what a riff is without listening to the different ways in which riffs are used in music, composing using riffs or playing riffs, is music learning without the music: it is *unmusical*. It is arguable that critical thinking and understanding can be developed and demonstrated only within a particular musical style, genre or context. It is the musical processes, procedures and characteristics of the genre or style that provide the parameters within which critical thinking and understanding can be demonstrated. Task 4.3 exemplifies this.

Task 4.3 Critical thinking and understanding in context

1 Select a style of music, other than western classical music, and play a few examples of it to your pupils.
2 In discussion with the pupils, help them to identify key aspects of this music in terms of:
   - its musical characteristics – what makes it 'sound' like jazz, rock, Indian classical, etc.
   - what characterises an effective performance within this style?
3 Use these discussions as a means of developing their critical thinking skills, particularly encouraging them to:
   - question any assumptions they may have about this musical style
   - reflect upon and justify their own beliefs and opinions.
4 Now ask them to compose a piece of music in this style. Frame the composing task as a form of 'musical problem solving' involving we described earlier as a 'conscious process of gathering, analysing, synthesising and evaluating'. You might offer them a number of musical ideas or starting points from which they select, according to their appropriateness for that style. Alternatively you could ask them to research the musical requirements for a particular rite or ceremony of the culture from which the musical style comes, composing something appropriate for it. Revisit the compositions as 'work in progress' in the context of a composing forum, where the children discuss each others' emerging compositions, drawing on aspects of critical thinking and understanding identified in this chapter.

Musical concepts, critical thinking and understanding

A second problem with the idea of knowledge as being 'fixed' is that it encourages a superficial and unmusical approach to the teaching of musical concepts. For example, pupils learn that a minim is worth two beats and that the rhythm 'crotchet–quaver–quaver' is a one-beat note followed by two half-beat notes. They may even – in the name of practical music-making – be taught to clap the rhythm from flash cards. However, the fact remains that the concept is being taught separately from any musical context which the learner recognises and can relate to and therefore be able to engage with *critically*. The musical concept or idea is not experienced within a musical context: it has no meaning and as it has no meaning it cannot be critically engaged with.

Musical ideas and concepts are re-realised, re-experienced and understood in different ways every time they are *personally experienced*. It follows therefore that understanding and knowledge is enhanced with each reacquaintance – one's 'knowing' of the concept is enriched with each renewed acquaintance through an individual and personal response to music. It is within this renewing and enriching of musical experience, where the same concept is met in different musical contexts that provides arenas within which *musical* critical thinking and understanding are developed.

Philpott (2007a) defines this kind of musical knowledge as knowledge 'of' music by direct acquaintance: 'it implies the building of [a] . . . *relationship* with the music (in the same way that we get to know a person or face)' (my italics). Such knowledge of music is gained from (and only from) immersion in music, responding to music through performing, composing and listening. Elsewhere, and drawing on the work of Keith Swanwick, Philpott (2007b: 4) argues that this knowledge 'of' music is 'at the core of why we engage with music at all, i.e. it means something to us!' Now carry out Task 4.4.

Task 4.4 Musical concepts in a musical context

Select a musical concept or idea that you wish – or ideally pupils wish – to gain an understanding '*of*'. It might be a compositional device such as a riff or ground bass, it might simply be the idea of repetition as a unifying element in music or you might wish to develop pupils' understanding of and ability to deploy common rhythmic patterns such as 'crotchet–quaver–quaver'.

Begin by finding five extracts which include the musical idea or concept which you wish to explore. These extracts should be taken from a wide range of music styles and genres with some being examples of music used for a particular social function (e.g. music for a celebration). Then take one of two approaches. Either:

- play the extracts and encourage the pupils to identify the common element unaided

or

- briefly outline the common element and then play the extracts with pupils' listening informed by that knowledge.

Now devise a series of questions about the music which encourage the pupils to evaluate the success of each extract both in terms of itself and in comparison with the others. The pupils should be encouraged to demonstrate those aspects of critical thinking and understanding outlined earlier in this chapter, particularly those relating to reflecting and justifying one's own beliefs and opinions.

These should include questions about:

- the effectiveness of the individual music examples in terms of what they set out to achieve

Task 4.4 *continued*

- the different ways in which the concept or element is exploited and the musical impact this has
- comparative evaluations of the music – which do they prefer or think works better and why? (It is important for the teacher to challenge children to justify their responses.)

Now ask the pupils to use the concept or idea in a specifically defined composing or improvising task. You need to define the nature of the composition either in terms of its function (e.g. music for an advert), its form and content or expressive effect. As in Task 4.3, it should pose a musical 'problem' which pupils solve through deploying their developing critical thinking and understanding skills.

Valuing personal knowledge

The purpose of the previous activities has been to demonstrate that the development of critical thinking and understanding is dependent upon an understanding by the teacher that knowledge is not just the kind that is 'out there' (the pre-cooked meal) but that people create (construct) their own personal reality, knowledge and truth *through* the act of thinking, reasoning and doing within real or authentic musical experiences and contexts. (To return briefly to the analogy of the meal, the learners gather the ingredients together themselves and create their own meal for a particular purpose.) These contexts can include the classroom, a church music group, a rock band rehearsing in a garage or studio or someone working individually creating music on a computer. We now need to add one more ingredient to this understanding which is that the construction of knowledge takes place not only within a musical context, genre or style but also, critically, within a child's own cultural, social, historical context – in other worlds the reality of their lives. Knowledge and understanding, truth and value are intimately bound up with the restrictions and opportunities endowed by a given context or situation. The personal development of (musical) knowledge – knowledge 'of' music – cannot be separated from a musical context and the lived reality of a learner's life. After reading the scenario in Box 4.1, carry out Task 4.5.

Box 4.1 Scenario

Tom is a beginner teacher committed to encouraging pupils to sing and to bringing into the classroom music with which they are familiar. With a 'challenging' year 9 class he decides to learn a pop song which they all know. Song sheets are prepared and he enters the classroom, confident that the lesson will work well because he is doing those things he has been told ensure positive behaviour. He leads the singing as a whole-class activity from behind the piano. The vocal sound is turgid and uncommitted and behaviour soon begins to deteriorate. He struggles through to the end of the lesson, disappointed and frustrated.

He speaks with a colleague who suggests that rather than teaching the song as a 'class' song (as a kind of community singing exercise), he should try to 'make it more of a performance occasion'. The next lesson he clears the desks to one side and places the

Box 4.1 *continued*

chairs in a double semicircle. He also arranges a backing track of the accompaniment. Rather than performing the song as a whole class, he teaches the class a few short riffs which fit with the backing track. Against the backing track and riffs he asks small groups to sing the song using a microphone and amplifier. The pupils react to this approach with enthusiasm and before long individuals are volunteering to sing solo, performing with commitment and a real sense of style.

They then discuss in groups different ways of performing the song: of phrasing, dynamics, how and when to 'bend' notes, how to elaborate the melodic line and to break into harmony. They perform their versions to each other, evaluating them according to *their* agreed criteria and what is and is not acceptable criticism (including the necessity of justifying what is said in musical terms).

Task 4.5 Valuing personal knowledge

In groups, and thinking back to the discussion about knowledge–learner relationships in the previous section, consider why both the pupils' attitudes and the lesson outcomes are so much better in the second lesson. Try to think beyond simply the resources used. It might be useful to consider the following issues:

- How has Tom connected what he does to the pupils' worlds outside the classroom – to their lived realities?
- In what ways are the children enabled to bring in knowledge from outside of school?
- How are the children involved in constructing their own learning and knowledge?
- What aspects of critical thinking and understanding identified at the beginning of this chapter are children able to develop and/or use in this lesson?

CRITICAL THINKING AND UNDERSTANDING: BRINGING IT TOGETHER

In this final activity you should draw on your developing knowledge of critical thinking and understanding to:

1 analyse a lesson you have previously taught
2 plan a new lesson which is specifically aimed at enabling pupils to develop their critical thinking skills and understanding.

As you work through Task 4.6, keep in mind the knowledge–learner relationships that are important to, and the teaching and learning contexts which best promote, critical thinking and understanding.

> **Task 4.6** Planning for critical thinking and understanding
>
> 1 Using a table similar to Table 4.2, take a lesson that you have previously taught and analyse the content, strategies and opportunities for learning against the conditions for, and characteristics of, critical thinking and understanding that we have explored in this chapter.
> 2 Now plan a lesson which is specifically focused on developing critical thinking and understanding. Describe the lesson in detail and then using the same table, indicate how the lesson addresses the conditions for, and aspects of, critical thinking identified within this chapter. Teach the lesson and then evaluate its success against the ideas and concepts explored in this chapter.
> 3 Return once more to Task 4.2. Add any further ideas about critical thinking and understanding that you have developed through completing this activity. In a discussion forum with other students, compare and exchange ideas about the nature of critical thinking and understanding and how you might enable children to develop and demonstrate their own critical thinking and understanding.
>
> Indicate how you might now change the lesson in the light of the understanding and knowledge of critical thinking and understanding developed in this chapter.

Table 4.2 Planning for critical thinking and understanding

Conditions for and aspects of critical thinking and learning	Lesson content, strategies, objectives and outcomes
Takes pupils' social and cultural backgrounds as a basis and starting point: pupils' lived realities	
Children are involved in constructing their own knowledge	
Knowledge of music is developed in a specific musical context	
Pupils engage with, analyse and evaluate music	
They consciously engage with their learning	
They question assumptions (their own or others')	
They justify their opinions drawing on their developing knowledge	
They adopt a systematic approach to problem solving	

SUMMARY

In this chapter you have thought about what is meant by critical thinking and understanding, and how this might be developed in the context of the music classroom. You have gained an understanding of how critical thinking and understanding is best supported and developed when pupils have ownership of their learning, and when music learning is given a context that relates to pupils' own lived realities. You will have developed an understanding that critical thinking *can only be* demonstrated through the *act* of making and responding to music within authentic musical contexts. Finally, you have analysed and developed strategies for supporting musical learning through critical thinking and understanding and vice versa. Most importantly however, you will have gained an understanding that critical thinking and understanding can lead to the realisation by the learner that they are empowered to change their world through engaging with knowledge.

FURTHER READING

Center for Educational Development in Fine Arts: http://finearts.esc20.net/music/music_strategies/mus_strat_crit.html. This American site looks at different approaches to music teaching and learning. It has sections on creativity, cooperative learning and the use of technologies in music teaching. The section 'Critical Thinking and Problem Solving' considers a range of teaching strategies for promoting critical thinking through music learning.

Schmidt, P. (2005) 'Music education as transformative practice: creating new frameworks for learning music through a Freirian perspective', *Visions of Research in Music Education* (special edition), January. Available at http://www-usr.rider.edu/~vrme/v6n1/vision/schmidt_2005.htm. This is an accessible, inspirational paper which argues 'that real learning takes place only if students and teachers alike are changed in and by the process of education'. It points the way to embedding critical thinking and understanding as a means of creating music education as transformative education.

Woodford, P. (2005) *Democracy and Music Education: Liberalism, Ethics, and the Politics of Practice*. Bloomington, IN: Indiana University Press. In this book Woodford considers the ways in which music education aims to support and promote democratic values, social cohesion and creativity. However, he argues that many present music teaching and learning practices are essentially undemocratic and argues for changes in music pedagogy and teacher education which might lead toward a 'liberal' music education.

Chapter 5   **Teaching creatively**

IAN SHIRLEY

INTRODUCTION

The very nature of human learning is founded on solving problems. As humans we invent tools, we create machines, we develop medicines, we devise artistic activities that express our innermost feelings, and we create games that channel our natural drive to win. In every aspect of life we are biologically predetermined to try to understand our world and, more importantly, we respond creatively to life's challenges. We try to intervene so that we gain control over our environment. We cut corners, we tell lies (little white ones, of course), we weigh up tricky decisions, we incorporate others' good ideas into our own work, and we work tirelessly to get the results we are content with, until a new issue arises and demands our attention. All of these acts can be considered *creative*. In this chapter we will focus on how your creativity as a teacher is important in promoting the creativity of your pupils in the music classroom.

OBJECTIVES

By the end of this chapter you should be able to:

- understand the nature of creativity;
- identify some key characteristics of teaching creatively;
- plan creatively for creative opportunities in music.

FINDING CREATIVITY

First, we need to explore what we mean by creativity (our own and our pupils') and under what conditions it takes place. Task 5.1 will help you begin to do this.

Task 5.1   Understanding the creative self

1 Draw up a list of the ways you have been creative today. Consider:
  - problems you have solved
  - experiences you have actively created for yourself
  - comments you have made
  - jokes you have told
  - journey routes you have taken.

Task 5.1 *continued*

2 Where did the solutions for these creative acts come from?
3 Try to determine the role that conditions such as confidence, happiness, fear, frustration, anger and determination had in these creative acts.
4 Consider the role that knowledge and understanding, conscious and unconscious thought, relevance, open-mindedness and play have had in the success of these creative acts.

Creativity is an active process and is sometimes thought to follow four distinct phases: preparation, incubation, illumination and verification (Wallas 1926). This is illustrated in Figure 5.1.

Another way of looking at the creative process, particularly in the arts, is described by the National Curriculum Council (1990: 48–49) as involving *exploring, forming, presenting* work in progress, *reforming, performing, evaluating* and *responding*. There is no set cycle here; an artist may begin at any point within the framework. A new work could begin in response to a major event, an existing work, or as an exploration of new ideas on an old theme. The process requires time to *explore*, time to *form* initial ideas, time to *present* initial ideas to others, a final *performance* or presentation, and an opportunity to *reflect* and *evaluate*. Task 5.2 is designed as a means of capturing and evaluating the creative process.

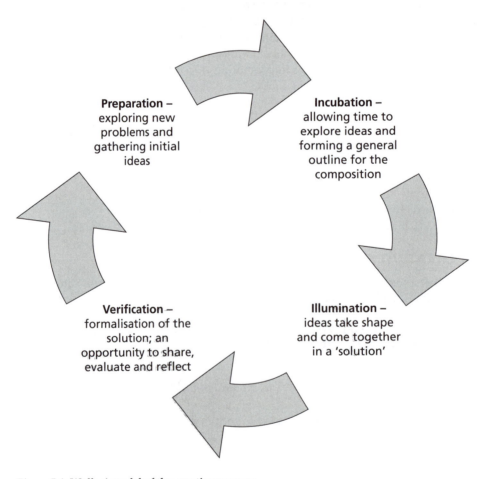

Figure 5.1 Wallas' model of the creative process
Source: Wallas (1926).

Task 5.2 Exploring the creative process in action

Works from other artistic disciplines offer a unique stimulus for creative music-making. With other student teachers choose a painting or sculpture (e.g. Munch, *The Scream* or Rodin, *The Kiss*) and then either individually, or in small groups, compose / improvise a piece of music in response. During and after the composition carry out the following:

1 Keep a composition journal (blog, scrapbook or diary) of how the piece comes into being.
2 Do your experiences of the creative process fit with the models proposed by Wallas and the National Curriculum Council? Use the headings from each to audit your experience in a table.
3 Compare notes with other student teachers. Are there any similarities and differences in your experiences of the creative process?
4 Compare any similarities and differences in your interpretations of the original stimulus.

Creative engagement and development is now widely regarded as a fundamental part of children's general development and, as such, it is embedded in current policy and strategy. Key to promoting creativity in the music classroom is the creativity of the music teachers themselves, and the rest of this chapter will focus on teaching creatively.

TEACHING CREATIVELY

A useful introduction to creativity in the secondary school is given by Fautley and Savage (2007). The authors explore general issues relating to creativity in secondary education and identify the importance of 'teaching creatively' as a necessary condition for 'teaching for creativity' and 'creative learning'. In short the creative imagination of the teacher is vital in promoting the creative learning and development of pupils.

'It would be hard to imagine a successful teacher inspiring their students towards creative processes and outcomes without some element of that creative spark being evident in their own teaching' (Fautley and Savage 2007: 21).

They go on to outline the features of teaching creatively which, among other things, include the following key characteristics:

- being an inspiration
- being able to stimulate curiosity
- finding your own teaching style to promote creativity.

It is the premise of this chapter that these characteristics provide a useful starting point for teaching creatively in the music classroom, and will form the basis of the remaining discussion.

Being an inspiration

We often consider that some teachers are more inspiring than others. The challenge for you will be to understand how you can inspire the creative musical lives of your pupils. In *A Passion for Teaching*, Christopher Day (2004: 40–41) includes some *memories* of inspiring teachers. Key characteristics of the teachers described in this brief section include:

- an ability to demystify and translate that which seems at first unfathomable;
- an infectious love for a subject;
- energy;
- commitment to a subject or discipline;
- commitment to the learning of the student;
- leaving the student with a feeling of exhaustion and exhilaration.

Consideration of these characteristics may well point to the inspirational qualities of your own *inspiring* teachers. They, in turn, may well become the models on which you base your practice. Now carry out Task 5.3.

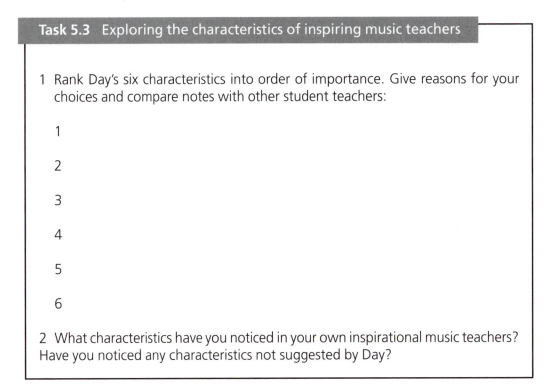

Task 5.3 Exploring the characteristics of inspiring music teachers

1 Rank Day's six characteristics into order of importance. Give reasons for your choices and compare notes with other student teachers:

1

2

3

4

5

6

2 What characteristics have you noticed in your own inspirational music teachers? Have you noticed any characteristics not suggested by Day?

Inspirational teachers inspire creativity through motivating and engaging their pupils in the discipline of music, largely by example. For these reasons the key to being an inspirational music teacher is an ongoing commitment to developing your understanding of music in all contexts.

In terms of knowing your subject, being an inspirational music teacher in the twenty-first century is a real challenge. No music teacher can know and understand all of the musical practices they are likely to encounter in school. While your knowledge and understanding will, in many cases, be transferable, the music teacher needs to develop an open attitude by being alert to the learning potential of all musics. Your chosen career is one which requires a lifelong commitment to learning, and a determination to be open-minded about future and current developments. Such openess is a prerequisite for creative teaching to promote creativity in the music classroom. As a teacher interested in the creative music-making of young people you should consider opportunities to extend your own musical horizons. Develop a lifelong approach to learning and adopt an attitude of the lead music learner in your school.

Another key feature of the inspirational music teacher is a commitment to reflecting on your practice and its effectiveness in inspiring your pupils. The categories in Task 5.3 can be used as part of your lesson evaluations to interrogate you being an inspiration in the music classroom. Furthermore, Task 5.4 will allow you to model the ongoing processes of openness and reflection in being an inspiration to your pupils.

Task 5.4 Openness and reflection in teaching creatively

Be sensitive and attentive to your daily musical experiences and consider the possibilities they bring for creative musical activity. Your own musical research can make a useful starting point, as in the following example.

Consider Rufus Wainwright's *Agnus Dei* (freely available on YouTube).
- Ask your peers or pupils to offer their initial thoughts on the piece. Deconstruct the music to discover how it tries to fuse eastern and western traditions of music. Ask why Wainright might have decided to bring these traditions together.
- Listen to other settings of this text in well-known works and compare the characteristic features.
- Encourage your pupils or peers to create their own settings of *Agnus Dei* in a fusion of eastern and western musical traditions such as raga, or using African drumming patterns and Blues.
- Be prepared to be controversial and thoughtful in your teaching. Compare images of the Lamb of God (i.e. agnus dei) and discuss with your students the nature of sacrifice – sensitive discussions of the nature of sacrifice in war could provide a deep insight into the inherent metaphor of the Lamb of God – the ultimate sacrifice.

Use this process to explore music that is new to you as a basis for inspirational classroom practice. What challenges does such 'openness' present to you? In what ways does such a process promote inspirational teaching?

Stimulating curiosity

Curiosity can be seen as the manifestation of the fundamental human instinct to make sense of the world. Curiosity involves exploration, discussion, research, enquiry, thought and the association of ideas; the essence of the creative process. Curiosity for music is often witnessed through informal learning where children are keen to play familiar riffs such as Mike Oldfield's *Tubular Bells* or *Smoke on the Water* by Deep Purple. It can also be associated with a sheer fascination after hearing certain sounds and musics for the first time. It is a subtle condition which requires flexibility on the part of the teacher, and while it is not always possible to know when curiosity will be aroused, it is possible to respond to it when it arises.

By and large ways of stimulating the curiosity of pupils are mirrored by the very same things that stimulate the curiosity of musicians themselves. In many cases a musician's curiosity is stimulated by a desire to solve a musical problem, for example, how to interpret a piece for performance, how to compose a jingle for an advert, how to set these words. The music teacher who teaches creatively constantly seeks new ways to set problems which stimulate the curiosity of their pupils. Now carry out Task 5.5.

Task 5.5 Stimulating and observing curiosity

1 Make comprehensive lists (a) of the ways in which your curiosity is stimulated as a musician, and (b) of any other musicians you know (dead or alive!). Share these with other student teachers and compare and contrast ideas.

Task 5.5 *continued*

2 Use some of these ideas to present your pupils with a variety of starting points for composition that could be open to individual interpretation: an image, a building, a video clip without the sound. Get them to consider events that have led to this image being produced and to suggest the kind of music that could be used to accompany it.

3 Try to find opportunities to surprise the pupils so that their initial interpretation is challenged. Video images such as *Powwaqatsi* (1988), by Godfrey Reggio and the opening sequence from *City of God* (2003) by Fernando Meirelles provide powerful images that should motivate your pupils to discuss difficult issues. Discuss how music has been used as a powerful tool of critical comment. Encourage them to be provocative and critical in their creative music-making.

In Activities 2 and 3, be attentive to the questions the pupils ask and where their curiosity is raised. Summarise your findings and report back to your colleagues.

Of equal importance to being able to stimulate curiosity is the ability of the music teacher to respond to the natural curiosity of their pupils. Many teachers are alert to children's curiosity and may, on occasion, abandon the planned curriculum altogether and respond to current events and issues as they arise. These events may be of international significance or they may arise out of comments asked by individual children. Such practice can be seen as 'the *roaming* curriculum', as it requires an immediate, unplanned response, picking up on children's curiosity just as international *roaming* picks up mobile phones.

Your ability to respond to your pupils' curiosity will sometimes depend on your confidence to let go of what you have planned. You will need to feel confident that you have the subject knowledge to support the pupils in the direction they wish to take and that the results will be worthy of the time taken up by the diversion. Experience suggests that such opportunities always have a positive effect on the children's perception of a subject. Now carry out Task 5.6.

Task 5.6 A case study in responding to curiosity in music

The pupils in one class had become animated in a discussion about the Lloyds TSB music, *Eliza's Aria*, from *Wild Swans*, by Elena Kats-Chernin. Rather than drawing the class back to the planned curriculum the teacher recognised that the pupils' curiosity had been raised and that there was much to be gained from following this line of interest. The teacher allowed the discussion to develop, asking the students to describe the main features of the song and to analyse why the song was appealing to the listener. The teacher found the advert on the internet and the class listened and appraised the qualities once again. They even sang along, enjoying the feel of the wordless melody on their throats!

The teacher encouraged the pupils to create their own piece of music which featured the main characteristics of the original. A simple descending chord pattern of D minor, C major and B♭ major was the given musical structure and the pupils were asked to think about developing the role of *texture*. The music was to last one minute: the length of the advert.

Task 5.6 *continued*

- Share examples of occasions when pupils have shown curiosity unprompted by the teacher. In what ways could you have responded to their curiosity to enhance their developing musicality?.

Finding a teaching style to promote creativity

The traditional view of teacher as expert places emphasis on the difference between the teacher and the taught. The teacher is seen as the fount of knowledge, pouring forth and filling the empty vessels of pupils' minds. The opportunity to experiment with sound, and the freedom to follow individual lines of interest, allowing pupils what we might call *agency*, is lost. Such a view of teaching and learning ignores what we know about how pupils construct knowledge out of interaction with their environment, in proximity to more knowledgeable others, and through a variety of activities including sensory experience and reflective thought. Part of the solution to providing agency may lie in recognising that we are all part of a learning community. In this way we can begin to provide the conditions necessary for the pupil to become *agents* in their own learning rather than subjects of our teaching. We help them learn from their experiences so that there is an increasing sense that they will initiate their own learning goals in the future.

Agency is about providing and managing autonomy. Like pocket money, *agency* allows for real decision making, within controlled parameters. Some decisions will prove wise, others foolish; agency involves an element of risk. Creative music projects, that promote autonomous activity, can help pupils to develop a spirit of perseverance, where challenges and disappointment promote creative invention and resilience. Allowing pupils to be active agents in their own learning involves a leap of faith on the part of the teacher, and a shift in 'concern for the curriculum' to 'concern for the pupil'. It requires a careful mix of autonomy and support, opportunity and challenge, knowledge and empowerment, and flexibility within clear objectives. Balancing these is tricky but, through honest reflection, the process becomes increasingly natural. Even so, just acknowledging your *will* to provide some autonomy represents a major step in giving your pupils agency.

Teaching creatively can promote agency and this involves balancing the initiative (agency) of the learner with the involvement of the teacher. Figure 5.2 illustrates a framework for discussing the role of different approaches to teaching in achieving such a balance. Task 5.7

Task 5.7 Finding a teaching style to promote creativity

Figure 5.2 represents four contrasting approaches to music education.

1 Discuss your experiences of each quadrant as a teacher and as a learner in music. In what ways do the opportunities you provide, and the opportunities you were provided, fit onto this diagram?
2 Discuss the benefits of each of the approaches described. In what ways can each approach support teaching creatively through balancing teacher intervention with pupil agency?
3 Reflecting upon your own practice, what alterations could be made to ensure that you are teaching creatively? Are all of quadrants represented in your teaching and do they need to be? How will your future practice be affected by this activity?

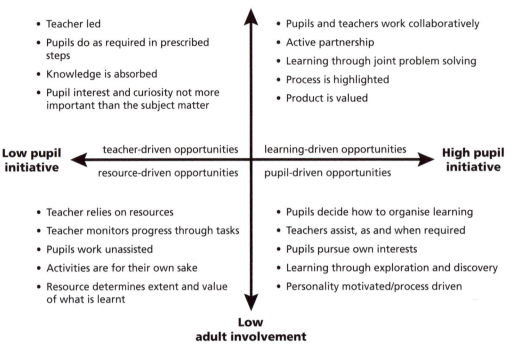

Figure 5.2 Finding a teaching style to promote creativity
Source: Barnes and Shirley 2005, adapted from Webster, Beveridge and Reed (1995).

will allow you to explore a teaching style to promote creativity, and if there are opportunities for you to embrace strategies for intervention and agency.

SUMMARY

In this chapter we have explored the nature of the creative process. We have also focused on three characteristics of creative teaching; being an inspiration, stimulating curiosity and finding a teaching style to promote creativity. By attending to these characteristics as student teachers, you can begin to develop the tools and strategies to facilitate the development of both your own and your pupils' engagement with the creative process. Any approach to teaching that is attentive to these characteristics will have a significant effect on how you plan and teach for creativity in the music classroom.

Music offers a unique arena for creativity. While the creativity you encounter won't often be large-scale, earth-shattering moments you can be sure that creativity often lies, subtly hidden, in the careful design and approach we take to music education.

FURTHER READING

Craft, A. (2005) 'Learning and creativity', in *Creativity in Schools: Tensions and Dilemmas*. London: Routledge, pp. 51–70. This chapter is an interesting analysis of the pedagogical issues which surround creativity in schools, for example, the role of teacher intervention and pupil agency.

Fautley, M. and Savage, J. (2007) 'Teaching for creativity' and 'Creative learning', in *Creativity in Secondary Education*. Exeter: Learning Matters, pp. 31–68. This book is a comprehensive exploration of current concepts of creativity. It offers much in the way of practical advice for the student teacher about teaching creatively, teaching for creativity and creative learning.

Philpott, C. (2007) 'Creativity and music education', in C. Philpott and G. Spruce (eds) *Learning to Teach Music in the Secondary School: A Companion to School Experience*, 2nd edn. London: Routledge, pp. 119–134. This chapter focuses on creativity in the specific context of the music classroom. As well as introducing theoretical perspectives, it offers some useful practical guidance, for example, when teaching composition and improvisation.

Chapter 6 — The integration of ICT in the music classroom

DUNCAN MACKRILL

INTRODUCTION

Technology is a very important aspect of twenty-first-century life. You may already have very good generic ICT skills and some experience in using music software but it is not uncommon to feel a little apprehensive about using specialist music technology in your teaching.

Music and technology are also very important to pupils; just talk to them about their musical interests and ask how many have their own portable music file players such as an iPod, or a mobile phone with the capability to play music. Some will also be very familiar with music software in their homes, creating and sharing their own music regularly. As music teachers we should recognise and engage with this interest as, when used well, music technology has the potential to stimulate and significantly develop pupils' learning.

Whether you already have considerable experience of using music technologies or are just beginning, this chapter is intended to guide you through a range of tasks to assist you to learn new skills and to consider how to effectively integrate ICT and music technologies into your teaching. The technologies are categorised as follows:

- generic ICT found in music classrooms, e.g. interactive whiteboard (IWB), computer, internet access;
- music-specific software and hardware, e.g. sequencing and scoring software, samplers, microphones and recording hardware, electronic keyboards;
- new and emerging technologies, e.g. Web 2.0, podcasting, Learning Platforms, hand-held technologies.

OBJECTIVES

By the end of this chapter you should be able to:

- understand how a range of technologies can be used to develop pupil learning in music;
- develop your own skills and experience of a range of technologies with the potential for use in the classroom;
- use technology appropriately as both a teacher and pupil tool in different situations and contexts.

KEY PRINCIPLES AND GETTING STARTED

The focus of this chapter will be on the use of software and computer-related technology, as these tend to be both the most prevalent and those that the majority of students have access to, both in and out of schools. However, there are many other technologies that you are likely to encounter, for example, electronic keyboards, samplers and recording hardware, which are all valuable and can be used effectively in the music classroom. Many of these are considered in *Learning to Teach Music in the Secondary School* (Philpott and Spruce 2007: 174–192).

Technology can be used in the classroom as a teacher tool – for example, for modelling, to aid demonstration, provide a backing for a class performance, or to record pupil work – or as a pupil tool where the pupils use it themselves. It is important that you know the technology you are using yourself before you begin to use it with your pupils. Therefore, this chapter focuses on developing your own skills and the use of technology as a teacher tool before moving on to pupil use.

Developing your technology skills in music is like learning an instrument – by doing a little and often these skills will develop steadily. At the start of an initial teacher education (ITE) course it is expected that an audit of subject knowledge will have been completed, including reference to music-specific ICT skills and experience. If you have not done this before, or it needs updating, you should do this in advance of undertaking the tasks that follow.

The National Curriculum for Music (QCA 2007c) states that the:

> study of music should include:
> 3f – the use of ICT and music technologies to create, manipulate and refine sounds

and that the:

> curriculum should provide opportunities for pupils to:
> 4a – develop individual performance skills, both vocal and instrumental, including the use of music technology.

> (QCA 2007c: 183–184)

Pupils are therefore *required* to use music technology at Key Stage 3 and it is important that you do too. However, this does not mean that you have to be a technology expert. It is a good idea to start with something with which you are familiar and are able to explore out of school, such as an audio recorder on a mobile phone or Finale's inexpensive 'Notepad' scoring software (download from www.finalemusic.com/notepad/ for around $10) before you move on to explore more complex technology such as digital recorders or sequencing software. Now carry out Task 6.1.

Task 6.1   School provision and identifying needs

Discuss with your mentor what technology equipment and software are available in the music department. Find out about how ICT and music technologies are currently used in specific units of work. Identify which technologies you need time to explore. Complete the table below, deciding on three short-term (i.e. in your current school) and three long-term areas for development:

Short-term area for development	Evidence
Long-term area for development	**Evidence**

GENERIC ICT FOUND IN MUSIC CLASSROOMS

Interactive whiteboards (IWB)

In the last few years the opportunities for communicating using the visual image have grown enormously and we are bombarded with high-quality visual images on a daily basis through television, games consoles, mobile phones and, particularly, the web. One only has to look at the popularity of video and photo-sharing websites such as YouTube and Flickr to realise the importance of the digital image across society. As teachers we need to use the technology available to engage our pupils, providing that, as well as increasing motivation, it aids and develops learning. An IWB provides significant opportunities to focus pupils' attention because the software can be operated from the board itself by the teacher and/or pupils, rather than from behind a computer screen where body language and gesture are lost and there is a physical disconnect between what is seen and heard. Resources can also easily be saved for use or editing with the same or different classes in the future. It can even diminish some classroom behaviour issues because the teacher is standing up, thus having a better view of pupils.

It is understandable that you may initially use an IWB as simply a way of projecting images onto a screen but the most important feature of an IWB is its interactivity, so it is important to begin to use this functionality as soon as possible in order to maximise the potential for learning. Box 6.1 describes ways of using an IWB.

Box 6.1 Examples of how an IWB can assist in pupil learning

- For actively involving pupils in making decisions and participating in using the IWB themselves.
- For modelling, presentation or tutorial, e.g. to show pupils how to carry out a particular task, or to use specific software.
- For concept consolidation, e.g. to show the structure or texture of a composition. Students can then make decisions themselves about how to arrange material, seeing it visually and listening to it at the same time.
- For use in a starter or plenary session to introduce, consolidate or summarise, e.g. using appropriate 'games' involving drag and drop, 'revealing' answers, virtual card sorts, concept maps, etc.
- For drawing graphic scores, diagrams, etc. on the IWB using different colours by the teacher and/or pupils during the lesson, which can then be saved. These can be displayed the following lesson, edited and/or printed as required.
- When using a score writer or sequencer and when notes, phrases or other objects are edited or dragged to different positions, aural feedback on the changes that have been made can be heard instantly.
- For emphasising points or features through the use of annotation tools and colour, e.g. related ideas or concepts can be indicated by the same colour.

As you begin to use the IWB remember that, as with any use of music technology, tasks should always be focused on improving learning, not on how to keep pupils amused. This can be a particular danger when devising materials for an IWB, so you must ensure that your activity is meaningful and musically relevant for your pupils.

For a listening activity using an IWB you might find appropriate videos on a video-sharing website. Insert the web address as a hyperlink into the lesson resource file but be sure to check in advance that the school firewall allows you to access the site you want to use. If it does not, you will need to look at saving the resource to a memory stick, etc. There are a number of software applications that can enable you to do this. You could then devise an interactive presentation which might involve questions, links to relevant websites and photographs and audio examples. You could also check iTunes or another legal portable music file repository for tracks you want to use. If you decide to transfer these files to a USB stick or burn them to CD/DVD, you will need to check that the computer that you are using to replay them supports the particular file format used. Now carry out Task 6.2.

Task 6.2 Effective use of an IWB

Identify a listening activity in an existing unit of work that you will teach and devise an interactive task to work on the IWB using a range of visual images, at least one quiz 'game' (for example, drag and drop answers) and at least one sound file. This might be a track you have downloaded to a portable music file player, a CD in the computer attached to the IWB, or an MP3 on a USB stick. Ensure that you use at least three ideas from Box 6.1.

Reflect on the impact of your use of an IWB on your pupils' learning.

MUSIC-SPECIFIC SOFTWARE AND HARDWARE

Audio recording

Portable digital recorders are becoming more common in music departments and many mobile phones now also have this facility. These technologies are quick, intuitive and can be used well in a music department but do not offer the editing requirements that are so often needed. For this, a good choice is the free audio editing and recording software for PC or Mac, Audacity: http://audacity.sourceforge.net/. You can find tutorials and a manual at: http://audacity.sourceforge.net/manual-1.2/index.html. If you have a laptop it will probably have an internal microphone but you will achieve better results using an external condenser microphone terminating in a lead with a mini-jack plug.

When recording, you should experiment with levels to determine how far you need to be away from the sound source. You will also need to remember to ask the pupils to introduce themselves (or do it yourself) so that you can identify who you are listening to when you replay it later.

For examination courses, it is more common to find pupils using multi-track audio recorders. These provide the potential for high-quality recordings to be achieved but most are quite complex and are often far from intuitive for the novice user. However, if you already have experience in using ICT in music you should make time to become familiar with the multi-track recording equipment in your placement school. For more information on audio recording hardware see Crow (2007: 187–188).

Video recording

The use of a camcorder (or even a webcam) to record pupils' work is a powerful and motivating use of technology. Using video in a plenary or for assessment is often underestimated but is a good tool for modelling and enabling pupils to see where they can improve, etc. It also provides a much more comprehensive record of pupils' work for review at a later time. Most pupils enjoy seeing themselves on video and this allows them to view their own performances – something they may never have seen before – but you must discuss the issue of permission to video in the classroom with your mentor as school policies and the agreements they have with parents and carers vary. Now carry out Task 6.3.

Task 6.3 Recording pupils' work

1 Identify and plan opportunities for recording pupils' work, either as finished pieces or work in progress.
   - Record the pupils' work into Audacity using a laptop or desktop computer and microphone. (If a portable digital recorder is available, you may use this to record and then transfer the audio (via a cable, Bluetooth or Infrared) into Audacity or other audio editing software.)
   - Save a copy before experimenting with some of the editing features, e.g. trimming the start and end of the recording, using normalise if it is too quiet, adding effects, etc.
   - Save your work for possible replay in a plenary session as a stimulus for discussion.
2 If you have access to video recording hardware and permission to video pupils, record examples of their work, either as finished pieces or work in progress.
   - Replay this work to pupils as part of a plenary and using assessment criteria, and ask pupils to peer assess the work.
   - Encourage comment on such things as how a pair or group communicate with each other and with their audience, their posture and how they might improve these aspects.

Using sequencers, score writers and MIDI files

As you begin to use a sequencer and score writer, you will need to consider which is appropriate to use when: if the primary purpose of use is to print music parts you should use a score writer; if it is to play as a backing for singing or performance, then you should use a sequencer as this will offer more opportunities for teacher control. For example, using a sequencer, you will be able to select sections to repeat more easily by quickly setting up markers and using the cycle function (particularly useful for improvisation sections, or learning new sections of music); transpose to a more pupil-friendly key (warning: do not transpose a drum or percussion part as the instruments used will change too); solo or mute particular parts according to need, etc. While these functions are often possible in score writers, it is far more difficult and not recommended in a classroom setting. Loop-based music creation software (e.g. Sony's Acid) can also be used effectively to create backings. You should also refer to Table 13.2 in Crow (2007: 186) for possible ways of using the music computer in the classroom.

Most sequencers and score writers can play, create or edit MIDI files but you will need to consider the issue of copyright as many MIDI files found online are unauthorised, i.e. the original composer or publisher has not given permission for this new 'arrangement' and as such the file is unlawful. However, you can contact the publisher to obtain permission. There are also many MIDI files that are permitted for educational use – particularly on education websites. MIDI files send data when it starts to play about the voices to use, volume, tempo, etc. and, if you wish to change these, you will need to delete this information first. This is normally carried out via the List Editor in a sequencer and you should check the manual on how to do this.

The activities in Task 6.4 should all be related to your teaching rather than being just exercises to complete, so think carefully about the resource you choose and the intended purpose.

Task 6.4 Three classroom tasks

1 Download the free MIDI and karaoke MIDI file player vanBasco from www.vanbasco.com/.
   • Find a range of suitable MIDI / karaoke files for classroom use (you can do this via 'MIDI Search' on the vanBasco webpage).
   • Download two files and use them with any of your current classes.
   • Discuss with your peers how successful your use of the files proved (e.g. via your university/college's VLE) and reflect on how you may use files in the future.
   (If you use a karaoke file and have access to a data projector you will be able to display the words to your class, synchronised with the MIDI backing.)
2 Create your own backing track using a sequencer for a rhythm 'call and response' exercise, improvisation passage, or other suitable activity for classroom use. This will enable you as teacher to select 'play' and then be hands-free to direct, assist or model to pupils. Your work may use some MIDI or audio loops if appropriate, for example, drum loops, and you might also include a number of original parts that you have created from scratch. Evaluate whether using a backing track was more effective than a 'live' accompaniment might have been.
3 Use a score writer to produce both the score and parts for an ensemble (about three or four separate parts). Either arrange an existing piece, or compose an original one for use in classroom performance or extra-curricular work. This could be for a whole class at Key Stage 3 or for a small group (e.g. of GCSE pupils). Evaluate the realisation of your score.

Developing ideas for units of work

Once you have some experience in using a number of technologies, you should think carefully about how you might use these as a teacher and pupil. Developing stimulating, achievable tasks for pupils using music technologies is probably your greatest challenge but it is important to include opportunities for this – the National Curriculum requires it. Some ideas are given in Table 13.2 in Philpott and Spruce (2007: 186). Here are a few more:

• Using GarageBand, Acid or another loop-based sequencer, pupils select a series of loops that can be combined to create a ternary form structure, or represent a mood or idea.
• Using a sequencer (or possibly a score writer), pupils compose their own Blues bass, melody or fill-in part(s) to pre-prepared chord and drum parts.
• Using keyboards with on-board memory tracks, and playing in real-time, pupils build up, track by track, the layers of a four-part rhythm pattern.
• Using a sequencer (or any other music software that can play synchronised video files), pupils compose their own soundtrack to a short advert or film clip.

As you plan your own learning tasks or adapt existing ones for use with technology, think carefully about the resources that are available and how you will use them. When devising learning activities using music technology, consider the following:

1   What do you want the pupils to learn?
2   What is the purpose of the task?

3　Which technology is best to use and is it for teacher [T] and/or pupil [P] use?

4　Is it integrated with the unit of work, enabling pupils to do something that would not be possible or would be less effective without the technology?

5　Does it allow for differentiation and give pupils at least some freedom to be creative or make their own choices?

6　How will the pupils demonstrate success and how will you assess what they have achieved?

7　What do the pupils need to know or be able to do before they can undertake the task?

8　Do they have this knowledge?

9　What is your back-up plan if the technology doesn't work?

10　Is all the technology/software functioning?

Now carry out Task 6.5.

Task 6.5　Integrating ICT into units of work

Identify one or more existing units of work in your placement school where the use of ICT and/or music technologies could be developed, or where you could enhance or develop student learning through its use in each of the following areas:

- performing
- composing
- listening.

Refer to the ten points listed in the text and suggest a particular technology or technologies (either hardware or software) that could be integrated into the unit. Carefully consider what the use of this technology will enable pupils to do that they could not do before. Develop your ideas into lesson plans and, if you have the opportunity, teach this in its revised form. Having taught your lesson, evaluate the success of the activity and pupils' learning.

- Was the chosen technology appropriate?
- What do you need to change for the future?

NEW AND EMERGING TECHNOLOGIES

In addition to many of the music-specific technologies already discussed, there is now a range of technologies based around Web 2.0 (e.g. social networking sites, wikis and blogs). These offer significant opportunities for pupils (and teachers) to network, share and collaborate, but care needs to be taken when considering using these with pupils. However, schools now have increasing access to school or local authority Learning Platforms that provide many of the opportunities for using Web 2.0 but in a 'safe', managed environment.

Handheld technologies (e.g. mobile phones, personal digital assistants (PDAs), iPods) are also beginning to be used more widely in education and should be explored. Mobile phones with voice recorders and cameras have the potential to be used more widely in education but you will need to check on school policies before using these in the classroom.

Podcasts – essentially where a digital recording is made and broadcast via an internet website using a syndication feed – are becoming increasingly popular and easier to make. For example, GarageBand for the Mac has this facility built in. If you have access to software to make and share podcasts or radio programmes think about using this as an outcome for pupils to demonstrate their understanding of what they have learnt. Your school Learning Platform may provide a vehicle for hosting teacher, or pupil, podcasts.

You are encouraged to explore the potential for using these technologies more fully during your training and beyond. When pupils have more ownership and influence over their work they tend to be more motivated and technology can be a good facilitator here. Now carry out Task 6.6.

Task 6.6   Pupils' ownership of their work

1   Adapt an existing unit of work such as one on film music or minimalism to involve pupils in 'collecting' their own sounds or images, via portable digital recorders or their mobile phones, both in and out of school. Alternatively (perhaps as part of a tutor time activity) ask them to collect sounds or images that represent or say something about their own identity. Give them a brief before they collect their resources. Pupils then import the audio/images into a sequencer, or other appropriate software* to be edited and used with other material.

2   When you have collected digital audio (or video) recordings of your pupils' work, ask your mentor what opportunities there are for accessing these easily and replaying them to pupils. For example, it may be possible to upload these to the school's Learning Platform or an education-based website like NUMU (www.numu.org.uk). This can be particularly valuable for storing important KS3, GCSE and other examination work in one location and enables teachers and pupils to access their own work both on and off campus to share with their parent/carer etc.

* This does not necessarily require expensive software and could be carried out using Audacity, Windows Movie Maker, GarageBand or, if working within tutor time, PowerPoint.

SUMMARY

The tasks in this chapter have provided you with some experience of working with a range of technologies, developing your own skills and gaining in confidence before using them in the classroom. You have identified the use of technology as both a teacher and pupil tool and considered how to make a task both stimulating and manageable. You will have some idea of the potential for using music technologies and ICT in the classroom and have begun to think creatively about how you use technology when devising learning activities.

If you began your training with relatively little experience in this area it is important that you start to become familiar with a range of music technologies as soon as possible. If your knowledge and expertise in music technology are already strengths then you have a distinct advantage and the challenge is to develop and devise stimulating learning activities that really do improve pupil learning. It is hoped that you will also share your expertise with those who have less experience. A virtual learning environment 'help' forum can be a good way of providing support when face-to-face contact is not possible, e.g. when you are on school placement. However, it is always important to ensure that you use technology when it enables you or your pupils to do something more effectively, or that they would not otherwise be able to do without the technology.

Lastly, one of the exciting things about music technology is that there is always something new to learn. Consequently, it should be an important aspect of your continuing professional development long after you qualify as a teacher.

FURTHER READING

Websites

Audacity tutorial: http://audacityteam.org/wiki/index.php?title=Tutorials

Computer Music magazine: www.computermusic.co.uk
A useful site with reviews of software, etc. and a range of useful free 'beginner' tutorials to download.

Gabcast: http://www.gabcast.com/
A free (or pay a small monthly charge for extra features) podcasting and audio blogging platform enabling you to record with your mobile (or VoIP), thus offering pupils the opportunity to do this with a mobile technology.

MIDI World: www.midiworld.com
Example of a MIDI file site for jazz and classical music.

Music Robot: www.musicrobot.com
Example of a MIDI file search engine – particularly for less popular titles.

NUMU: www.numu.org.uk/
Free, online safe space for music education where students (and/or teachers) can upload audio files of the music they compose or perform, in or out of school.

PC Publishing: www.pc-publishing.com/
Range of useful guides on audio recording, Cubase Logic, etc. and a 'Get Creative . . .' series of practical projects and tutorials for Cubase and Logic.

Wells Cathedral School: www.imusic.org.uk/
Free downloads of the Virtual Javanese Gamelan and West African Drumming module.

Software

Audacity: http://audacity.sourceforge.net/
Free audio editor and recorder for PC or Mac.

Finale: www.finalemusic.com/notepad/
'Notepad' music notation software for PC or Mac – around $10.

Sony Acid Xpress: www.sonycreativesoftware.com/download/trials/acidxpress
Free loop-based software for PC.

vanBasco: www.vanbasco.com/
Free MIDI and karaoke file player for PC.

Books and resources

Block, S. and Murray, A. (2006) *Interactive Whiteboard Activities for Music*. Stevenage, Herts: Badger Music.

Clyde, S. (2006) *MIDI Sequencing – Made Easy*. St Andrews, Fife: Softplanet Ltd.
Book, video tutorials and a copy of Cubase LE for PC or Mac.

Kitchenham, A. (2007) *Classroom Resource Pack for Cubase 4.1 and Cubase Studio 4.1*. Steinberg.

Paterson, A. and Ley, B. (eds) (2004) *Ideas In Music Out: Using Technology in Music Education*. Matlock, Derbyshire: National Association of Music Educators.

Chapter 7   Assessment for learning in music

MARTIN FAUTLEY

INTRODUCTION

Assessment is a key topic in music education today, and one important aspect of it forms the focus for this chapter, that of assessment for learning. To begin to make the most of the potential that assessment for learning offers you and your pupils, it is important to understand that formative assessment is not a 'bolt-on' extra, but is integral to the very way you plan learning, and interact with your pupils.

So, what is assessment for learning? Assessment for learning, also known as formative assessment, commonly abbreviated to AfL, is a key feature of the work of all teachers. It was defined by the Assessment Reform Group (ARG):

> Assessment for learning is the process of seeking and interpreting evidence for use by learners and their teachers to decide where the learners are in their learning, where they need to go and how best to get there.
>
> (ARG 2002: 2)

AfL is often informal, involves conversations, helps pupils to improve and is integrally bound up with your normal day-to-day work as a music teacher; indeed, 'to teach *is* to assess' (Swanwick 1988: 149).

OBJECTIVES

By the end of this chapter you should be able to:

- understand what assessment for learning entails;
- understand how it differs from assessment *of* learning;
- understand the role of feedback;
- know how to use the key AfL tool of questioning;
- be able to use AfL strategies in your lessons.

THE NATURE OF ASSESSMENT FOR LEARNING

Philpott (2007a) discusses key aspects of AfL, drawing particularly on the work of Black *et al.* (2003), and thinking about the very nature of what AfL entails is a useful place to begin a consideration of the topic. The first thing to do is really unpick what is meant by the terminology 'assessment for learning', understand precisely what it is, and how it is of use to both pupil and teacher. To understand assessment for learning, and how it differs from assessment of learning, we need to get to grips with the middle word from each, 'for' and 'of'. Assessment *of* learning (AofL) looks over past achievement and summarises it. It can be thought of as looking backwards, and paying no attention to what is coming next; it is separated from the learning experience, and often occurs at the end of a learning episode. Assessment *for* learning, on the other hand, is integral to learning and teaching, and its purpose is specifically to look forward to the next stages in learning. Figure 7.1 shows a graphical representation of these differences.

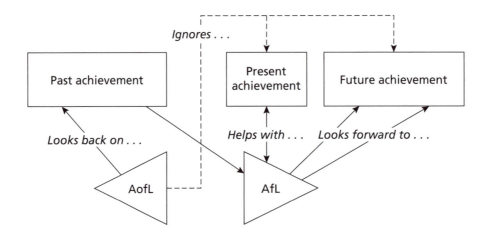

Figure 7.1 AofL and AfL

Figure 7.1 shows AfL being linked to present and future achievement, whereas AofL, by and large, ignores these, and looks back over prior work. For you as a teacher, this distinction is key and one where we need to be really clear about the terminologies employed. What this shows is that the *purposes* of formative and summative assessment are different. Put simply, summative assessment is something which is normally 'done to' pupils, and occurs at a specific time, where its purpose is to summarise achievement and will often result in a grade, mark or level. Formative assessment differs from this in that it is 'done with' the learners while they are in the process of learning, might not necessarily lead to a mark, but does involve conversing with the pupils about what they are doing now and what they need to do next in order to improve their work. This makes formative assessment an active and intentional component of what is going on in the classroom, and is 'any assessment for which the first priority is to serve the purpose of promoting students' learning' (Black *et al.* 2003, cited in Philpott 2007a: 211). Now carry out Task 7.1.

Task 7.1 Reflecting on AfL

Think back on your development as a musician. What was said to you that helped you improve? How was it said? Was it demonstrated? Who said it? How did they say it? In what ways do you think it might count as assessment *for* learning?

THE ROLE OF FEEDBACK AND LEARNING DIALOGUES

When you have a conversation with pupils while they are working, what you are most likely to be doing is giving them feedback. This is a key component of AfL, but is such an everyday occurrence in the music classroom that, as one music teacher observed, 'It doesn't feel like

I'm doing assessment'. Yet that is precisely what is going on! These conversations that you have with pupils will be focused on improving learning, and what results is a dialogue where three phases are involved:

1 You need to intervene in the process of learning or music-making.
2 You elicit information from the pupils (individually and collectively) regarding what they are doing, and develop your understanding of this from work-in-progress performances and dialogues.
3 You proffer feedback in the form of suggestions, tease out understandings, and help the pupils towards higher achievement.

To do this is to be undertaking assessment *for* learning. You are actively making professional judgements on a number of levels, and building on the responses you get from the pupils to help them with knowing what to do next. This all seems very straightforward, and goes some way towards explaining why the teacher above felt it did not seem like assessment. But to do this effectively involves some very careful planning and thought on your part. Let us look more closely at the phases involved, and what exactly you will be doing in each.

Intervening

In a KS3 class there will be a number of groups working simultaneously, and so you will be moving between them. This means that groups might be working for a proportion of their time away from your direct supervision; you will want to maximise the impact of your interventions, so think about how best to find out what you need to know. This begins with you deciding what you do first, stop the group, or listen for a while and then intervene at a natural break. According to the Office for Standards in Education (Ofsted), 'Good teachers judge carefully when to interrupt or intervene, so as not to disturb the flow of activities' (Ofsted 2003: 4).

Eliciting

Having ascertained from listening to their music what the pupils are doing, you can then proceed to elicit information from them. This is a dialogue, and so you will need to think about what it is you are trying to find out! Remember that your pupils are working with sounds, and so it may not be appropriate for them to explain orally what they are doing. Far better for you to say 'Show me, don't tell me'. This does not mean pupils do not have to explain, but this can come later.

Giving feedback

Here you proffer feedback as to what can be done to improve. Any assessment involves an emotional component, and so the key notion here is to be constructive, and work with the pupils. This can require careful handling to steer their work into directions which you feel are appropriate. Now carry out Task 7.2.

Task 7.2 The role of feedback

Think about the three phases of intervening, eliciting and giving feedback. Next time you plan a lesson involving a practical activity indicate on your lesson plan opportunities to intervene, elicit responses and offer feedback. Make a conscious effort to involve these three as you talk to pupils. Ask yourself:

Task 7.2 *continued*

- *Intervening*
  - How will you intervene: stop; wait; interrupt; listen?

- *Eliciting*
  - What do you want to know?
  - How will you find it out? (Maybe 'Don't tell me, show me'?)

- *Giving feedback*
  - Do they know what a good outcome will sound like?
  - Have you modelled it for them?
  - What will you do and/or say to help them?

Consider the effectiveness of the language you have used in your post-lesson evaluation.

THE KEY AFL ROLE OF QUESTIONING IN THE LEARNING DIALOGUE

The questions you ask throughout will be key to your understanding of what is going on, and, as questioning is a key component of AfL, needs to be thought about carefully. Philpott (2007a: 213) observed that it is worth 'spending effort framing questions which are worth asking'. In the process of giving feedback described above this is vital. It may seem when you observe music teachers that the questions they ask arise spontaneously; however, the teacher concerned has experience to draw upon, and you may find it helpful to plan. 'Questions which are worth asking' may not flow, and it is useful for you think about what the answer might be before you ask the question! This means you need to have considered what it is that the pupils are doing, and frame your questions accordingly.

You may have met Bloom's taxonomy (Bloom 1956) in your professional studies sessions (for an overview see Zwozdiak-Myers and Capel 2005: 111). In this the first three 'layers' are considered lower-order thinking, the final three higher-order thinking. Although there can be problems of a too-rigid application of this taxonomy with regard to creative activities, it does present a useful classification system for thinking about developing questions for use in music lessons. Box 7.1 shows some question stems derived from Bloom's taxonomy which may be of help in planning worthwhile questions.

Box 7.1 Question stems for use in music lessons

Knowledge	Can you show me what you are doing . . . ?
	Can you play me that bit where you . . . ?
	Can you remember how to . . . ?
Comprehension	Can you perform that bit where you . . . and tell me what is going on at that point?
	What is the idea behind . . . ?
Application	How will you play the next bit where . . . ?
	Can you play for me an example of . . . ?

Box 7.1 *continued*

Analysis	What is going on in that bit where you . . . ?
	Can you explain (or show me) what went on when you were doing that middle bit where . . . ?
	Can you show me (or explain) how what you are doing differs from her part where . . . ?
Synthesis	What do you think it would sound like if you joined that bit with . . . ?
	What would happen if you were to put your ideas together with hers . . . ?
Evaluation	Why do you think that was successful at the point where you . . . ?
	If you were to change any part of your piece, which would it be . . . ?
	Can you tell me (or show me) why you . . . ?

Using these question stems, you can tailor questions to suit the learning your pupils evidence. Research has shown than many teacher questions tend to be of a low-level recall type, so it is worth preparing in advance. Now carry out Task 7.3.

Task 7.3 Questioning

1 Using the question stems listed in Box 7.1, plan a series of questions for a forthcoming lesson you will be teaching. Design questions which lead pupils into the higher areas of Bloom's taxonomy. Plan your questions using Box 7.1.
2 After you have undertaken this during your lesson, reflect on how it went.
   • Did you ask 'good' questions?
   • Did the pupils cope with this?
   • Did you have to improvise additional questions?
   • If so, how effective were these?
   • What sorts of questions worked best? Why?
3 Now think about the questions you have just been asked in the task above – which areas of Bloom's taxonomy (Box 7.1) are they concentrating on?

As AfL involves a dialogue with pupils, it is not a matter of working your way sequentially through a predetermined list of questions, but of interaction. In other words, 'what learners say and do is then observed and interpreted, and judgements are made about how learning can be improved' (ARG 2002: 2). So, gathering information about your pupils is not enough in itself, you then need to act upon it, *and* help the learners know how to act upon it.

SUCCESS CRITERIA

Sharing notions of quality in music lessons goes to the very heart of AfL. As one of the classic formative assessment texts notes, 'The essential conditions for improvement are that the student comes to hold a concept of quality roughly similar to that held by the teacher' (Sadler 1989: 121). To do this means you need to think about what you want to happen. A starting point for this in your music lessons is to separate process from product, and learning from doing, and then think about what you are looking for in each. Doing this involves creating criteria for successful learning and successful doing; these are *success criteria*. Now carry out Task 7.4.

Task 7.4 Success criteria 1

Think about a practical music lesson you will be teaching soon.

- What will a good musical outcome be?
- What will it sound like?
- Have you modelled it with the pupils?
- Do they know what a high-quality musical outcome will be?
- What do you want the pupils to do?
- What will they learn?
- What do they need to know and be able to do before they can undertake this task?

Using this information, write some success criteria for various aspects of this lesson.

Success criteria are quite hard to write at times, as they need you to think about things from the perspectives of the learners. Let us consider this from the perspective of a KS3 group composing lesson. You will have given the pupils a starting point for their composing; let us take the example of composing for a film clip of a train departing from a station, and pulling through a cityscape. As you are planning the lesson, you can plan for some AfL to take place too. Possible areas to think about include the questions listed in Box 7.2.

Box 7.2 Planning learning

Lesson elements: planning questions	Enacting questions
What does group work entail?	What can I do to help with it?
What do I want the groups to achieve?	What is the most effective way I can let them know this?
What does the process of group composing involve?	How do I know that they know this? What do I need to do to help with it?
Does the process matter?	Hopefully – as you want them to get better at it! What does this entail?
What sort of piece of music am I looking for?	Given the resources they have, what will a good outcome sound like?
How long do I want them to work at it for?	Is one lesson enough?
How will I know when to stop this?	What will groups do if they finish at different times?
How can we share our pieces of music?	Performing? Audio recording?

For these questions to become effective AfL you need to take heed of pupil responses, and re-engineer your lessons accordingly. This involves planning for subsequent lessons as a result of what has gone before. Your responses to dialogue, the way you develop your ongoing units of work, are as crucial a part of effective AfL as asking good questions. Now carry out Task 7.5.

Task 7.5 Success criteria 2

Using the music for a train in a cityscape example from above, write some success criteria for the composing task in this lesson.

Revisit Task 7.4 for help with this.

PEER AND SELF-ASSESSMENT

'Self-assessment is essential to learning because students can only achieve a learning goal if they understand that goal and can assess what they need to do to reach it' (Black and Wiliam 2006: 15). For practical music lessons this means that students need to understand what it is that they are meant to be doing, and, crucially, what they need to do in order to be able to achieve a successful outcome. This links closely with the notions we have already looked at of *quality* and *success criteria*.

Practical teaching example

In a KS3 group composing lesson, you may have set up a task which involves a number of separate components:

- structural features (e.g. beginning, middle, end)
- specific content (e.g. music for a project on ocean music)
- musical features (e.g. ostinato)
- control features (e.g. instrumental proficiency, such as playing chords on a keyboard).

For effective self-assessment to take place, the pupils need to be aware of these features, and know something about what they need to do in order to incorporate them into their piece of music. This means they can take their own learning and doing forward, without the teacher leading them every step of the way. Peer-assessment is a part of this process as it involves the pupils talking with each other about their music, and doing so using their own terminologies. This distributes AfL among members of the composing group, and acts both as a valid way of working in its own right, and as a way of facilitating movement towards each individual taking responsibility for their own learning. Now carry out Task 7.6.

Task 7.6 Self-assessment

Design a simple self-assessment sheet which your pupils can fill in during your next lesson.

- What prompt questions will it contain?
- What areas do you want them to focus on?

Task 7.6 *continued*

- Will you distinguish between questions which are about *doing*, and those which are about *learning*?
- How will the questions relate to the learning outcomes and success criteria for the lesson?

EVIDENCE

Evidence in music is likely to include pupils evidencing their understandings through attainment; as we have seen, this can be musical, as well as verbal. A key source of evidence is therefore going to exist as sounds. Modern technology makes recording sound a simple process, and does not require complex or expensive equipment. Finishing each lesson with a work-in-progress performance which is recorded allows the next lesson to begin with playing back what was done last time. This is a good AfL tool in its own right, as pupils can use listening to recordings as both an aide-memoire, and something to critique. Musical evidence can build up over time so that you can view progress being made. Recordings can also form the basis for focused questioning, be used to take learning forward, and provide a platform for saving musical performances (Savage 2007). Used this way, musical evidence can be a powerful tool. Now carry out Task 7.7.

Task 7.7 Assessment evidence

What sources of evidence do you have upon which to base your assessment judgements?

Here is a starter list:
- recordings: audio and video
- pupil workbooks
- computer programs – saved work
- your notes
- pupil information sheets
- conversations with pupils
- discussions with instrumental teachers
- information from parents.

Are there any others you can add to this list?

THE FORMATIVE USE OF SUMMATIVE TESTS

Grades, marks and National Curriculum levels have not been mentioned in this discussion of AfL. Doubtless you will be asked to provide summative assessment data, often in the form of National Curriculum (NC) levels, at various points. It is important to note that summative assessment, although obviously important, will not by itself help pupils to improve. What will be needed is specific, targeted feedback to pupils which tells them what they need to do to improve, and how they can go about doing it. Many teachers talk of having an 'assessment lesson' at the end of a unit of work, as though that is the only time that assessment takes place, in other words they have turned 'their own on-going assessment into a series of "mini" assessments each of which is essentially summative in character' (Harlen and James 1997: 365). The message of this chapter is that this is not the case! While you may want a specific event, for example, an end-of-unit performance, to be the subject of formal assessment, you will have been making hundreds of AfL judgements en route to this endpoint. Remember Swanwick's (1988) 'to teach is to assess'! However, summative assessment results do have a place in AfL and it is worth noting that

> using the terms 'formative assessment' and 'summative assessment' can give the impression that these are different kinds of assessment or are linked to different methods of gathering evidence. This is not the case; what matters is how the evidence is used.
>
> (Harlen 2006: 104)

The *formative use of summative assessment* 'builds on marks and grades given, and entails entering into a dialogue with pupils about why they got the result they did, and what they need to do in forthcoming work in order to improve their results' (Fautley 2008: 1). Now carry out Task 7.8.

Task 7.8 The formative use of summative assessment

- Look at summative assessment data that the music department has for the pupils you teach. What form does that data take? Marks, grades, scores, NC levels?
- What picture does it give of the pupils in question?
- What can you do to provide summative assessment data to contribute to the overall profile of a pupil?
- What will you do with this data to help progress pupil learning?

SUMMARY

In this chapter we have discussed the main differences between AfL and AofL. You have planned for using dialogue with pupils to inform your teaching, and, linked with this, thought about the central role of feedback, and the importance of asking good questions. We have also considered the various forms evidence takes when considering learning in music. Having worked through this chapter, hopefully you now understand that AfL is a way of teaching and learning where the focus is on taking learners forward. For you, as a beginning teacher, AfL, used properly, is a powerful way of helping your pupils towards realising their potential.

FURTHER READING

Assessment Reform Group: www.assessment-reform-group.org
This website contains useful information about formative assessment, has a number of important publications available to download, and links to writing about assessment.

National Association of Music Educators (NAME): www.name2.org.uk
This website contains information on music education generally, with links to publications concerning assessment.

Black, P., Harrison, C., Lee, C., Marshall, B. and Wiliam, D. (2003) *Assessment for Learning: Putting It into Practice*. Maidenhead: Open University Press. Written by some of the key figures in AfL research, this book describes how a group of teachers put AfL strategies into practice, and the ways in which this helped raise achievement. It is helpful in giving real-life examples from the perspective of classroom practitioners.

Fautley, M. and Savage, J. (2008) *Assessment for Learning and Teaching in Secondary Schools.* Exeter: Learning Matters. This book covers a range of assessment strategies and procedures, including AfL, and is written especially for student teachers.

Part 3   Broadening your perspectives

Chapter 8   Continuing pupils' experiences of singing and instrumental learning from Key Stage 2 to Key Stage 3

JULIE EVANS

INTRODUCTION

'They do nothing at primary school.'

Janet Mills (1996: 7) observed that this was a common perception of many secondary music teachers and suggested that many pupils experienced 'an unsuccessful start to secondary music education'. In their research over a decade later Marshall and Hargreaves observed that 'most [secondary] teachers still appear to find it necessary to "start from scratch" ' (2007: 78). It is important to understand that your pupils have had very varied musical experiences at Key Stage 2 but that *all* pupils bring a wealth of musical experience to the secondary school. This might have been gained in school or out of school and in a formal, non-formal or informal context. This chapter will explore how secondary music teachers can find out about and build on their pupils' prior experience of singing and instrumental playing.

> ## OBJECTIVES
>
> By the end of this chapter you should be able to:
>
> * understand what kinds of musical experiences your pupils bring to the secondary school, including an awareness of some KS2 initiatives relating to singing and instrumental learning;
> * know 'where your pupils are at' in terms of singing and instrumental learning;
> * develop strategies to build on what they have learnt and ensure progression in singing and instrumental learning from KS2 to KS3.

EXPERIENCES OF SINGING AND INSTRUMENTAL LEARNING THAT PUPILS BRING TO THE SECONDARY SCHOOL

All of your pupils bring experiences of singing and instrumental playing to their secondary school. In curriculum music lessons they have had an entitlement to 'sing songs, in unison and two parts' and to 'play tuned and untuned instruments' as laid out in the statutory National Curriculum for Music at Key Stages 1 and 2. However, this entitlement does not ensure that all primary pupils have been engaged in *sustained and effective* vocal and instrumental learning. A number of important initiatives have been developed to try to improve pupils' experiences.

Singing

Singing is an important and intrinsic part of growing up and your pupils will have sung with their parents and carers, in the playground, on the terraces of football matches, in choirs, shows and churches as well as singing along to their favourite bands. In the Music Manifesto Report no. 2, *Making Every Child's Music Matter*, it is suggested that: 'Singing . . . is where most children's musical journey begins' (DfES 2006a: 30).

The government has funded a major initiative to try to develop 'a singing nation'. 'Sing Up' is a national programme of singing activity for primary school children which aims to ensure that good-quality singing is central to young children's lives in primary schools, in the home and in the wider community. Now carry out Task 8.1.

Task 8.1 Using 'Sing Up' resources

Access the Sing Up website: www.singup.org.
- Look at the section called 'Teachers and Music Leaders'.
- Access the Song Bank. (These songs have been suggested for primary pupils to sing. However, virtually any song can be used with pupils at different key stages.)
- Choose three songs from the Song Bank which complement your year 7 units of work and which you feel will be engaging and stimulating for your pupils.

Prepare to teach each song in the following ways:
1 Download the resources that come with each song (e.g. lyrics, audio tracks, songsheets, activities, lesson plans).
2 Listen to the songs and ensure that you are fully familiar with, and confident in delivering, the melody and lyrics.
3 Decide how you will teach the lyrics to your pupils. If they will need to see the words on a sheet or screen, then prepare the necessary resources.
4 Listen to the echo tracks which you and your pupils can listen to and copy and decide how you will use the tracks to teach the songs to your pupils.
5 Decide whether you will need to play an accompaniment or use a backing track and then practice the accompaniment or rehearse with the backing track.

- Encourage pupils to give a performance of each song, either in a formal context like a concert or in a more informal context such as performing to another class.

Instrumental learning

For decades pupils have had the opportunity to receive instrumental tuition in schools but the percentage of pupils taking advantage of these lessons has been limited (around 8 per cent of the school population in 2002). Study Box 8.1 and then carry out Task 8.2.

Box 8.1 Wider Opportunities programmes

- In the White Paper *Schools Achieving Success* the government pledged to ensure that 'Over time, all primary pupils who want to will be able to learn a musical instrument' (DfES 2001: 12) and this became known as the Wider Opportunities Pledge.

Box 8.1 *continued*

- Wider Opportunities programmes were instigated which were intended to give as many pupils as possible access to specialist instrumental tuition during KS2 for a trial period (see Chapter 17 of *Learning to Teach Music in the Secondary School*: Philpott and Spruce 2007).
- The government's Guidance on the Music Standards Fund Grant 2008–2011 stated that: 'By 2011 we believe that all primary school pupils who want to **can** have the opportunity to learn a musical instrument' (Department for Children, Schools and Families (DCSF) 2008: 1).
- Many pupils at your secondary school will have had the chance to take part in Wider Opportunities-style programmes. Hallam *et al.* (2007) suggested that over 50 per cent of KS2 pupils were involved in a Wider Opportunities programme in 2007–2008.
- Pupils will have learnt to play an instrument (or to sing) in large groups, whole classes and even whole year groups. Pupils may have learnt to play instruments from a variety of cultures, orchestral instruments or more unusual instruments (such as ukuleles) or may even have made and played junk percussion instruments.
- Whatever instruments they have played, pupils will have substantially developed their musical experience. In addition to developing technical skills pupils will have developed their aural skills, ensemble skills and, probably, some ability to read notation(s). The programmes may have also involved the pupils in complementary activities such as singing, kinaesthetic activity, improvising and composing. Most importantly, the pupils' musical experiences will have gone far beyond just developing instrument-specific skills.

Task 8.2 Building on Wider Opportunities-style programmes

- Investigate what KS2 Wider Opportunities-style programmes are being offered to pupils in your feeder primary schools.
- Briefly note what instruments pupils have had a chance to play, whether your pupils have learnt to read notation(s) (e.g. stave notation, rhythm grids, tab) and what other activities they have been involved in (e.g. class singing, improvising).
- Devise a whole class improvising activity which allows each pupil to demonstrate their musical knowledge, using pupils' own instruments wherever possible. The activity could focus on rhythmic improvisation (e.g. in a samba piece where small groups of pupils or individuals could improvise on just one note in sections indicated by a break) or melodic improvisation (e.g. in a piece which uses a restricted range of pitches such as a pentatonic scale where the class could set up layers of riffs over which groups or individuals could improvise).

Pupils will also have had the opportunity to play instruments outside of school. Hallam *et al.* (2007) found that 13 per cent of KS2 pupils received specialist instrumental tuition in addition to those involved in Wider Opportunities programmes. Some pupils will have had private instrumental tuition. Others will have taken part in commercial instrumental lessons such as those offered by Yamaha Music Schools, learnt alongside others in brass bands or cadet bands, learnt from friends or taught themselves. Do not dismiss any sort of instrumental learning. For instance, pupils who have learnt from friends or have taught themselves often have highly developed aural skills, since much of their learning will have involved playing by ear. Informal learning is becoming an important model of musical learning within the curriculum at KS3 with initiatives such as Musical Futures (see Chapter 1) and you will need to build on similar models which are being adopted at KS2.

As Paterson and Davies (2005) suggest,

> when children move on . . . [we] need to take into account all the integrated experiences that the children bring with them from their home, school, social and musical life to enable continuity and progression.
>
> (Paterson and Davies 2005: 5)

KNOWING 'WHERE YOUR PUPILS ARE AT' IN TERMS OF SINGING AND INSTRUMENTAL LEARNING

It is your responsibility as a secondary music teacher to know where your pupils are at in order to ensure progression in their musical learning. Coll (2007: 231) states that many secondary music teachers simply ask their pupils about their prior experience during their first music lesson in year 7 but suggests that this can be problematic since pupils may have little to report. This is reinforced by Marshall and Hargreaves (2007):

> Many pupils . . . were anxious not to discuss the music they took part in out of school, preferring to keep their musical activities 'out of school' and their music 'in school' quite separate.
>
> (Marshall and Hargreaves 2007: 74)

It is certainly not a good idea to 'survey' your pupils in a first music lesson since you want to begin to build strong relationships with your pupils and establish your music classroom as an active, purposeful place where music-making is central.

The most effective way to assess your pupils' prior experience is to involve them in singing, playing, composing, reviewing and evaluating within a carefully constructed initial KS3 unit of work.

An initial unit should allow pupils to work creatively and imaginatively on open-ended tasks rather than being constrained by more common closed tasks, typically based around notation or the elements of music. Very importantly, this will allow you to assess your pupils' creativity as well as their skills. In the Secondary National Strategy for Music resources (Unit 1: 11) there are some suggestions for how to encourage pupils to work with abstract ideas. See Task 8.3.

Task 8.3 Gauging your pupils' prior experience

Access the Secondary National Strategy for Music website: www.ks3music.org.uk. Read the section in Unit 1 (starting on page 11) headed 'The tradition of working with abstract musical ideas'. The task is constructed around the concept of working with abstract musical ideas using a page from a composer's notebook.

1 List the range of musical starting points in the example (e.g. scales, words) and suggest what you could glean about your pupils' prior experience as they explore these ideas on voices and/or instruments.
2 Create a similar page to that from the computer's notebook to use as the main focus of an initial unit of work using voices and instruments for your year 7 pupils.

From the start of KS3 encourage your pupils to use their prior instrumental and vocal experience in their curriculum lessons. Pupils may be able to bring their own instruments to curriculum lessons. Your school may be able to provide a small number of larger instruments to be used in curriculum lessons, e.g. bass guitars, cellos. It can be very depressing to observe a class of pupils all struggling to compose using keyboards when in fact many of the pupils could be working more effectively on instruments that they have already learnt to play, either formally or informally!

You will want to record and celebrate your pupils' music-making during their transition from primary to secondary school, both in and out of school. This requires collaboration with primary colleagues. Some schools have devised musical 'passports' which pupils carry with them from each phase of their education. See Task 8.4.

Task 8.4 Musical passports

Discuss with a music coordinator from one of your feeder primary schools how you can devise a musical passport for your pupils to support their transition from Key Stage 2 to 3. Think about what you might want to include within the passport, e.g. What musical opportunities has the pupil had within the KS1 and KS2 curriculum? What instrument(s) has the pupil learnt to play within or beyond their primary school? What singing activities has the pupil taken part in within or beyond their primary school? Has the pupil gained any grades or other recognition (e.g. Music Medals) for their instrumental or vocal learning? Does the pupil wish to begin or to continue instrumental or vocal tuition at their secondary school?

STRATEGIES TO ENSURE PROGRESSION IN SINGING AND INSTRUMENTAL TEACHING FROM KS2 TO KS3

Singing

It is important that your pupils 'sing in solo or group contexts, developing vocal techniques and musical expression' as required in the National Curriculum for Music (QCA 2007b). The Ofsted Annual Report of 2004–2005 stated: 'Pupils need to engage in good quality singing more frequently at Key Stage 3 . . . Singing should be a regular activity and not restricted to particular schemes of work' (Ofsted 2005: 2). In some units of work the use of singing may be obvious (e.g. a unit of work on song-writing) but try to include singing even where its use may seem less obvious. For example, in a unit of work about dissonance, pupils can learn very effectively about the *sound* of intervals through vocalising them.

If your pupils are to sing regularly, then you need to be confident in leading singing. Always practise singing a song before you use it with a class and ensure that the song is within your own vocal range and that you have memorised both the melody and lyrics. Aim to get your pupils singing as well as possible, with good intonation and projection. You should build in unpitched warm-ups before singing. This will look after your pupils' voices but, by not using pitches, can encourage those pupils to participate who think that they can't or won't sing. Drama teachers often use exciting vocal and kinaesthetic warm-ups which can transfer very well to the music classroom. See Task 8.5.

Choose your repertoire carefully. Pupils at the start of KS3 are young adolescents and you need to ensure that the lyrics, pitch and vocal range of songs are appropriate. Few boys' voices will have broken by the start of KS3 and you may be surprised that pupils in year 7 can sing comfortably at quite a high pitch. If you think that your pupils need to see lyrics to support their learning, then use a data projector or interactive whiteboard to display the lyrics so that pupils look up when they are singing.

Task 8.5 Warm-up activities

Observe a drama teacher working with a year 7 class. Make brief notes of any vocal and kinaesthetic activities that the teacher uses and ask their advice about other possible warm-up activities.

- Devise a warm-up activity to use with your year 7 pupils before they sing.

You may want to use contemporary songs. The tastes of year 7 pupils range from R'n'B to new rave to musicals and it is important to include songs from a wide range of styles. Using a familiar song can allow pupils to start from where they are at before you lead them to encounter less familiar music. For instance, *Seven Nation Army* by The White Stripes could be taught as a song in its own right but uses a simple repeating bassline which could be used to introduce pupils to this concept in other styles of music, such as a Baroque ground bass.

Performing contemporary songs provides opportunities to link your pupils' singing and instrumental learning. Pupils will gain a huge amount from singing and playing whole class arrangements. This will mean making arrangements which are tailored to your pupils, with vocal and instrumental parts that challenge the most experienced and include the least experienced. See Task 8.6.

Task 8.6 Arranging a song

Choose a contemporary song which demonstrates a musical device (e.g. *Stop the Clocks* by Oasis features simple piano figurations; *Foundations* by Kate Nash uses basic root position triads). Make an arrangement of the song for a whole year 7 class, including vocal and instrumental parts tailored to your pupils. Teach the song using some of the advice from the previous section:

- Ensure that the song has suitable lyrics and is within your own and your pupils' vocal range.
- Practise singing the song before you use it with a class.
- Memorise the melody and lyrics.
- Devise a related vocal warm-up.
- Use a data projector or IWB to display the lyrics.
- Teach the song to your pupils by modelling it to them.
- Ensure that you can confidently direct the singers and instrumentalists.

If you are not a confident keyboard player you can create backing tracks for songs using sequencing packages (e.g. Cubase or Logic) or you might use a free online karaoke player such as vanBasco (see Chapter 6).

You may involve your pupils in singing beyond the classroom in activities such as choirs and shows but a 'singing school' is best established through regular enjoyment of singing within the curriculum.

Instrumental learning

You need to consider how group learning, similar to the Wider Opportunities programmes offered at KS2, can be continued at KS3. You may be able to rekindle pupils' enthusiasm to play instruments that are available at your school and which they have played before. Pupils may be able to start learning new instruments that they have always wanted to. You may need to work in collaboration with instrumental or workshop leaders (see Chapter 9). Familiarise yourself with published resources to support learning in large groups. See Task 8.7.

Task 8.7   Group instrumental teaching

Find a published resource which is designed to support group instrumental learning (e.g. *Standard of Excellence* published by Kjos Music Company; African drumming resources on www.african-drumbeat.co.uk).

- Use ideas from the resource to plan a very first instrumental lesson for a large group of instrumentalists on instruments that you know how to play.
- Consider strategies that will make the lesson run smoothly such as managing the instruments, ensuring that pupils make sounds on the instruments as soon as possible, allowing for different competences and making sure that the pupils understand what and how to practise before their next lesson.

(Remember that you are aiming to enthuse a large group of pupils who have had *some* prior experience.)

Making links between pupils' music-making in different contexts is challenging but essential. Mills (2007: 17) describes two young cornet players who saw their instrumental lessons as completely separate from their curriculum lessons. She is clear that the players could have made more musical progress if their education had helped them to bring together their learning from the classroom, instrumental lessons and informal contexts. 'Teachers can give children opportunities to talk about, and to show, the music they do out of school, and try to build on this' (Mills 2007: 17). As a start, you need to find out as much as you can about your pupils' experiences in instrumental lessons and out of school and encourage them to use their own instruments in curriculum lessons.

SUMMARY

In this chapter you have gained understanding of the kind of musical experiences your pupils bring to the KS3 classroom and awareness of some of the current KS2 initiatives relating to singing and instrumental learning. You have considered how you might know where your pupils are at and how you might develop strategies to ensure progression in their singing and instrumental learning from KS2 to KS3. It is reassuring to find that Marshall and Hargreaves (2007: 78) state, 'that the liaison between schools on either side of the "great divide" has improved in recent decades' and that this 'has removed much of the pre-transfer anxiety'. In terms of singing and instrumental learning you will need to develop this liaison and collaboration with colleagues such as music coordinators in feeder primary schools as well as with instrumental and singing teachers, choir and ensemble conductors and workshop leaders to facilitate a smooth transition from KS2 to KS3 for your pupils (see Chapter 9). Strategies for developing liaison and collaboration are well established, such as welcoming records from primary schools and other sources, encouraging year 6 pupils to visit your school and music department to take part in musical activities, visiting feeder primary schools (perhaps with some of your pupils) to lead or collaborate in musical activities or to work with musicians of all ages in community projects. Continuity in your pupils' singing and instrumental learning needs to be considered over a period of time. As Marshall and Hargreaves (2007) state:

> To 'transfer' to a new school is an event which happens quickly, but to 'make the transition' from primary to secondary school is a process which may take far longer.
>
> (Marshall and Hargreaves 2007: 79)

FURTHER READING

Allen, P. (1997) *Singing Matters*. London: Heinemann.

Hunt, P. (2001) *Voiceworks: A Handbook for Singing*. Oxford: Oxford University Press.

Both of these resources contain photocopiable support materials and songs in a range of styles to help teachers deliver singing in the KS3 classroom.

Mills, J. (2007) *Instrumental Teaching*. Oxford: Oxford University Press. Janet Mills' book seeks to help teachers teach in a manner that is true to the nature of music and what musicians do – in other words, to teach musically.

Chapter 9 Musical collaborations with other adults

KATHERINE ZESERSON

Team-working (with local musicians) is helping a lot at our school . . . it's as though one team is in operation.

(Secondary Head of Music)

(All unreferenced quotations are drawn from collaborative projects that the Sage Gateshead has led in secondary schools in the North East and Cumbria between 2005 and 2008.)

INTRODUCTION

Music is a truly living subject – your pupils are likely to be passionate about it, engaged with it and listening to it in their own time. Our challenge as music educators is to harness that connection and inspire pupils to move from passive to active in their musical lives, or to move from the familiar to the unfamiliar in their choices.

According to the National Curriculum of 2007, one of our main aims as music educators is to broaden the 'range and content' and the 'curriculum opportunities' afforded to our pupils. Within the section entitled 'Curriculum Opportunities' it is clearly stated that pupils should have opportunities for 'working with a range of musicians'. Developing musical collaborations with other adults – within and without the classroom – is an exciting and rewarding way of broadening your pupils' experiences, as well as your own, and can enrich the cultural life of the whole school. Ann Orfali (2004: 3) states that: 'There is widespread recognition that active partnerships between an artist and school can offer long-term development opportunities.'

Increasingly, local authorities, music venues and other professional music organisations are actively reaching out to engage with schools, and the government's most recent guidance to local authorities (DCSF 2008) strongly encourages music services to develop wider delivery partnerships in order to ensure that all children have the widest range of opportunities. Collaboration with other musical partners should form a key element of your teaching toolkit, ensuring full inclusion of all your pupils in a range of high-quality, inspiring and diverse opportunities.

OBJECTIVES

By the end of this chapter you should be able to:

- understand the value – to pupils, to your school and to you – of musical collaborations with other adults;
- have an insight into what is involved in planning and facilitating successful collaborations;

- have concrete ideas for collaborations and strategies for making them happen, including who you might work with and where you might find them;
- understand how collaborations might be built into schemes of work and assessment.

WHY MUSICAL COLLABORATIONS WITH OTHER ADULTS?

[This collaborative project] has given the students the confidence to perform on their own and in an ensemble. As a teacher it's great to see different ideas used to create composition/performance. Some of [the visiting artist's] ideas, I have already used with other pupils – with much success – to do with listening skills, rhythm skills, composing/improvising skills.

(Secondary music teacher)

Working with other adults in the classroom and enabling your pupils to get involved in musical collaborations in the wider community broadens their range of musical experiences and connects them to a range of role models, while at the same time offering you the opportunity to develop your own skills through learning from other practitioners. As well as deepening musical understanding, working with other adults presents pupils with different styles of leadership and different approaches to music-making. This is relevant in areas of music practice where you are specialist and confident just as much as it is in areas where you are less knowledgeable.

For example, if classical choral conducting is your particular area of expertise, then working with a vocal ensemble that specialises in jazz or improvised repertoire, perhaps learned primarily by ear, offers you and your pupils the chance to both build on your existing knowledge base and develop new skills. On the other hand, working with a professional classical choral conductor will enable your pupils to deepen their learning of something they are already familiar with, and reference their school experience to a professional model of the same music practice. As Lewis (2005) suggests:

This has to do with understanding what interests you and what you are good at doing, knowing what you do and what you do not do. I am convinced that the deeper your work comes from inside you the more likely it is to impact on others.

(Lewis 2005: 37)

Now carry out Task 9.1.

Task 9.1 The benefits and issues of collaborative practice with other adults

Audit the collaborative practice that you have been involved in as:

1 a pupil
2 a student
3 a musician (e.g. you may have been used as a 'visiting musician').

In each case, describe the process and the product. For example, when you were a pupil did your curriculum music teachers ever bring in workshop musicians? What sorts of activities were you involved in? Did this result in any sort of performance?

- Draft some bullet points of the benefits and issues of collaborative practice with other adults.

Musicians who work primarily as performers (or in other aspects of the industry), and less as teachers, will bring a fresh language of expectation and behaviour from their professional lives into the school environment. They will develop a different kind of relationship with your pupils, particularly if the collaboration has a performance or recording outcome; sharing their real-world professional practice with your learners. Professional role models help to broaden pupils' horizons and aspirations, and this can be particularly helpful in inspiring less engaged or confident pupils. Finding collaborating partners whose musical qualities are different to your own, or who come from other cultural backgrounds, can help you ensure that all your pupils find inspiration in a musical role model.

> When the musicians came they actually give you an opportunity to do different stuff like rapping, beat boxing, singing song lyrics, making your own raps up, working as a team, like helping you do stuff in teams . . . they actually let us pick our groups, we called our group 'DX' it means 'Degeneration X'.
>
> (Year 7 pupil)

When working with an unfamiliar musical genre or cultural form it is always inspiring and challenging to involve an expert in that practice. Hearing a high-quality, authentic performance of the music engages pupils in a richer understanding of what they have been studying; participating in a workshop or master class led by an expert ensures they have a sound grasp of the practice they are engaged in; learning via collaborative leadership broadens their experience of practising, learning or understanding music-making.

> The kids seemed to get more in that one hour than they've done in many lessons. Some of the most difficult year 8 pupils were brilliant at rapping and performing 'new monkey'. They would normally never volunteer for anything.
>
> (Secondary music teacher)

There should be learning opportunities for all collaborating partners. It is important to agree your role in the collaboration so that expectations are clear on all sides. You should understand whether continuing professional development for you will come from shadowing or observing your collaborator, or from co-leading, whether there will be specific training sessions for you and other colleagues to participate in and so on. It may be useful to identify some specific learning points you hope to explore yourself, and equally for the musicians with whom you'll be collaborating to do the same.

> I have learned so much from [the music teacher]. She's so good at finding the right level of challenge for each pupil in her class, while at the same time keeping the music exciting and sustaining a real sense of collective endeavour.
>
> (Visiting musician)

> We should be doing more of this [listening exercises], it's quite challenging to describe how a piece of music makes you feel and it changes the perception of what you are listening to, opens up the ears . . . I have since been using call and response games when the class are flagging, it helps to stimulate their minds and focuses the group.
>
> (Secondary music teacher)

Now carry out Task 9.2.

Task 9.2   What collaborations would you like to engage in?

1 Think of a class you have taught, or are currently working with. What specific areas of their music learning do you think would benefit from collaboration with

---

Task 9.2 *continued*

other adults? What would you expect your pupils to gain from the experience? How would a musical collaboration help deliver the curriculum? What would you expect to be different about the learning experience?

2 Thinking about your own musical skills, what specific area of your performance practice would you like to develop in collaboration with others? Is there a specific area of your music teaching you'd like to develop in collaboration with others? Why? What would you hope to gain from the experience?

WHERE DO YOU FIND COLLABORATORS?

We've been exploring a new model for working with video and sound installation, linking art and music students from four Cumbrian communities along the West Coast Railway Line. They've been working with their teachers and with visiting artists to create a DVD, using film taken from the cab of the West Coast train. Our music students have created the soundtrack, producing composition work which has involved collecting, recording, manipulating and editing sound sources, linking real sounds and synthesised sounds using 'Soundabout', a surround sound environment. The students have had very little music technology experience before, but are responding superbly, finding unusual sources for their sound generation – such as the [Ordnance Survey] grid reference for Sellafield!

(Project director)

Clearly, your choice of collaborators will depend on what you are trying to achieve, although sometimes you will want to react opportunistically to an offer from a touring company, a local arts venue or your local authority Music Service.

Touring musicians are increasingly interested in, and available for, musical collaborations. The best way to get them involved is to form positive relationships with venues near you, with your local Arts Council and local authority arts teams, so that they know you and your school and think of you when they are booking artists. Telling them that you are interested in a particular thing – for example, if you are focusing on Caribbean music for a period of time, or looking at approaches to improvisation – can help them find opportunities for you.

Making relationships with locally based professional musicians is an excellent way of ensuring sustained opportunities. Many Music Services are now working with a wide network of professional artists across their regions and can help you get in touch, as can your local or regional MusicLeader, Creative Partnerships or Arts Council (see web links at end of chapter).

Your own school staff may include musicians that you are unaware of – ask around in the staff room and put out invitations for them to come forward. Equally, there may be parents with musical skills you can draw on. Involving musicians from across your school community in pupils' learning can have all kinds of positive impact on people's perceptions of one another, and help foster a culture of mutual support and exploration.

The performance was really quite an awesome experience . . . it was done at the Theatre . . . The children had to go somewhere and the parents had to go somewhere different, and it wasn't in the school hall, and that gave it a status, the fact there were children from other schools there, everybody listened and it became a real community event.

(Parent)

Now carry out Task 9.3.

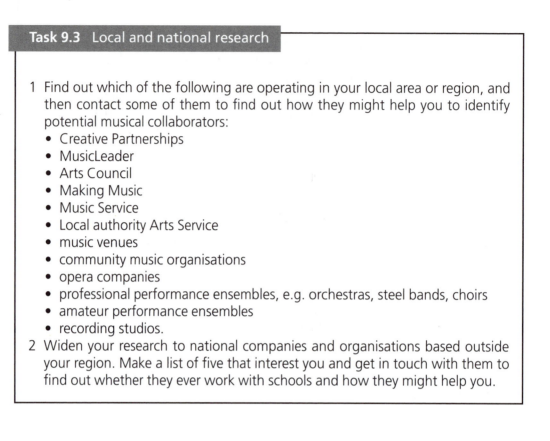

Task 9.3 Local and national research

1 Find out which of the following are operating in your local area or region, and then contact some of them to find out how they might help you to identify potential musical collaborators:
  • Creative Partnerships
  • MusicLeader
  • Arts Council
  • Making Music
  • Music Service
  • Local authority Arts Service
  • music venues
  • community music organisations
  • opera companies
  • professional performance ensembles, e.g. orchestras, steel bands, choirs
  • amateur performance ensembles
  • recording studios.
2 Widen your research to national companies and organisations based outside your region. Make a list of five that interest you and get in touch with them to find out whether they ever work with schools and how they might help you.

WHAT MIGHT YOU DO TOGETHER?

> Music, and young people's interest in music, is diverse. Multi-stranded music delivery therefore is the most effective approach to meeting and developing the learning potential of these young people and ensuring all young people achieve.
>
> (Project director)

Successful musical collaborations come in all shapes and sizes, ranging from one-off school-based workshops through to long-term extended community programmes. They can involve devising, improvising, composing, rehearsing, performing, reviewing, recording, analysing, coaching, teaching and celebrating. They can include a wide range of models, for example, a series of school-based workshops leading to performance; participation in a community-wide, multi-element project involving out-of-school sessions; co-led activities; visitor-led activities; master classes; seminars and discussions; composition and recording of film music, and more.

Teachers and musicians who are used to working in different contexts may not speak the same practice language, or operate with the same underlying assumptions about classroom management, communication, behaviour expectations and so on. Of course this diversity of approaches is one of the most vivid and energising aspects of collaborative work – for pupils and adults – and you would not want to iron out all these differences. At the same time it is important to talk about your ideas and assumptions to ensure that you make the best of your collective skills and experiences. Focusing your planning conversations on outcomes for pupils will help with this. And take risks – let the programme include challenges for you as well as for your pupils, and let your pupils see you learning alongside them.

> The fact that the teachers were in the circle alongside the children, that was really nice and I sensed that there was a bit of 'Oh!' [from the children], you know, here's a thing

where they [the teacher] are learning from somebody else, so the role of the teacher became participatory instead of saying 'Johnny sit down!' So when Johnny or whoever was talking when I was about to say something, it was me who would say 'Can we have quiet now' and it wasn't the teacher, the teacher was in the circle. And I think that's good for people and young people to see, how their teacher is around that, I actually think it makes that bond a bit stronger in a kind of, they're both in a learning situation and maybe it equalises things a bit. That was definitely happening.

(Visiting musician)

You are the trusted guide and broker. You know your pupils and know your school. You can open doors to new musical worlds through setting up collaborations, working alongside your pupils; and then you can support, reinforce and maximise the value of the opportunity. See Task 9.4.

Task 9.4 Exploring collaboration

You will need a musical partner for this activity, preferably someone from a different musical background.

1 Spend a couple of hours together sharing musical ideas and playing. Make sure that this session includes some activities you're both confident in and some activities you each find challenging. Take turns teaching or leading each other.
2 Discuss the session, exploring how it felt to lead and to learn, and how it felt to make music together. Identify a musical idea or activity that you both found inspiring.
3 Take that idea or activity as the theme for a workshop with a group of pupils. Plan the workshop together, making sure that you both lead some elements as well as supporting the other's leadership.
4 Review the planning process. How easy or difficult was it to agree on the core theme? How easy or difficult was it to agree on roles? What would make it easier?
5 Lead the workshop together, and then review together. Was the co-leadership fluid? Did you support each other effectively? What happened if one of you wanted to divert from the plan? What worked well in terms of student experience and outcomes? What worked less well? What did you learn from each other? How could the workshop have been improved?

HOW DO YOU CREATE AND DELIVER SUCCESSFUL COLLABORATIONS?

Successful collaborations are built on mutual respect and shared values. You need to be clear about your expectations and approaches, as well as being flexible and responsive to the different practices and perspectives other musical partners will bring to your pupils. The first step in developing a successful collaboration programme is to establish a clear purpose. You might want your pupils to develop more focused performance skills; to develop ambitious improvisation skills; to learn more about a specific tradition, e.g. South Asian music; to make closer connections with their local music community; to find out more about careers in music; to develop their collaboration and team work skills; to understand more about arrangement and harmony and so on. Having established a purpose (which might contain several integrated elements), you can then start to research the right musical partners.

You may have a very tight budget to work with, or even none at all, so you will need organisational support and partners too. See Box 9.1.

Box 9.1 Scenario

Pupils work on a year-long song-writing programme, aimed at developing composition skills, writing for context, arrangement, performance and understanding of song within two or three different musical traditions. In term two it is planned that a local musician will come into school to lead a series of composition workshops, leading to a performance of a new song cycle. Pupils prepare for this in term one by researching and securing 'commissions' for theme songs or songs to be used by local organisations – a playgroup, a sports club, a youth centre. Once a term pupils go out of school to master classes, talks or workshops led by artists performing at local venues, coupled with attending their concerts. In term three pupils take their songs back to the commissioning venues and perform or teach them, as well as producing recordings for the commissioners.

Take the time to work through in-school negotiations beforehand – does the timetable need to flex to accommodate your ideas? Who do you need on board to support you – with enthusiasm and energy as well as resources? What other activities can dovetail with your programme in order to create a larger, shared celebration? It is also important to prepare pupils, making sure that they understand and are interested in the programme and have taken on board any logistical or other changes to normal routines.

Moser and McKay (2005: 15) list the following features of a positive learning environment for a workshop and these all need to be considered:

- simplicity
- variety
- feel good factor
- a group that is open and receptive
- a sense of achievement and ownership
- attractive equipment
- enthusiastic, non-judgemental leadership
- a flexible plan with sensible activities
- musical progression and layering
- laughter to free the spirit and loosen inhibitions
- safety
- risk
- challenge
- individual space
- light
- patience
- team work
- clear communication
- well-explained boundaries
- listening.

Planning with your chosen collaborators is where the fun really starts. Agreeing shared goals for the work and acknowledging your own mutual learning needs as well as intended pupil outcomes will really strengthen your creative partnership. Make sure you and your collaborators allow time for mutual reflection and evaluation as the programme unfolds (if it is running over time) or at the end of the session (if it is a one-off). Review progress against your agreed milestones and take note of the unexpected outcomes that may be emerging. Openness and honesty are important – you and your collaborators can always learn more. Now carry out Task 9.5.

Task 9.5 Setting up a collaboration programme or activity

1 Write an outline for a collaboration programme involving a year 8 class for two terms. Make sure you have thought about the following:
   - *Purpose*: What do you and your pupils want to achieve through the programme?
   - *Objectives and targets*: How will you define programme milestones? How will you assess pupil progress and achievement? How will the programme or activity relate to the curriculum?
   - *Content, roles and responsibilities*: Who will you work with? What will your roles be in the classroom? In organising the programme? What kinds of activities will take place? What will the different strands of musical activity be? How will they be drawn together?
   - *Logistics and practicalities*: Where will the work take place? When will it take place? What practical negotiations or arrangements do you need to make in and out of school? What's the critical path to making the project happen?
   - *Resources*: What musical resources will you need? What's the budget for the programme and how will you fund it?
2 Discuss your plan with your Head of Music and enlist her/him in helping you to realise it.

SUMMARY

Musical collaborations with other adults enrich and challenge pupils and teachers alike, and can kick-start profound, long-term culture change in your school as well as providing galvanising moments of fresh inspiration. As Ann Orfali suggests:

> Schools are enlisting the help of creative partners, recognizing their expertise as a valuable resource to harness pupils' imagination. Through an enriched curriculum, innovative teaching and learning styles are engaging pupils, including some of those children at risk from exclusion.
>
> (Orfali 2004: 19)

Successful collaborations are based on shared goals, excellent planning, open-minded reflective practice, honest, respectful communication – and enthusiasm. Making excellent music with others – adults or young people – is a joyous experience that affirms community. Your pupils will remember this feeling long after the detail of the programme fades from memory, and the values of inclusion, respect and mutual achievement that underpin really great music-making will stay with them for life.

> These young musicians have grown enormously in confidence and are now taking charge of their own learning. They rehearse unsupervised at lunchtimes and compose their own pieces. They perform professionally and with a real sense of self-esteem. They respect each other and work well as a team. If what these students have achieved in a few months could be replicated across the school it would have a huge impact on the ethos of the school and the attitude of students to their learning and to each other.
>
> (Secondary Head of Music)

FURTHER READING

Arts Council England: www.artscouncil.org.uk

Creative Partnerships: www.creative-partnerships.com
These organisations are a source of ideas for musical and artistic collaborations and also possible funding.

Musical Futures: www.musicalfuture.org.uk
Musical Futures is an exciting, accessible method for enabling student teachers to lead their own learning in a range of partnerships. Philosophy, research findings and lesson plans, etc. are available from the website.

MusicLeader: www.musicleader.net
MusicLeader is the national professional development network for musicians, teachers and others working with young people and music. Membership is free. The website offers a wide range of training opportunities as well as a database of musicians available by region.

Music Manifesto: www.musicmanifesto.co.uk
The Music Manifesto website is a comprehensive, lively place to stimulate your creative thinking about music teaching and learning.

Moser, P. and McKay, G. (eds) (2005) *Community Music: A Handbook*. Lyme Regis: Russell House. This is an authoritative survey of approaches to community music practice.

Chapter 10   The integration of music with other subject disciplines, particularly other art forms

JONATHAN BARNES

INTRODUCTION

The medium of music is sound. This obvious truth is often missed by non-musicians (and sometimes music teachers) as they plan the inclusion of music into cross-curricular themes, projects or sessions. While the discipline of music can be a powerful lens through which pupils can understand and express their own experience of the world, in the real world music is experienced in a multimedia, multimodal context (e.g. concert, film, dance).

A cross-curricular approach to education has a long history. It was implicit in aspects of ancient Greek and medieval Chinese views of education where drama, music and literature were combined. Cross-curricular experience, at least for younger pupils, reappeared in the writings and work of eighteenth- and early-nineteenth-century progressives like Rousseau, Pestalozzi and Froebel. In the UK it was re-examined in the twentieth century a number of times, prior to becoming an important consideration in the 1960s and 1970s as a response to the Plowden Report (Central Advisory Council for Education 1967). Today, government legislation and advice has secured its re-examination across the key stages in the twenty-first century.

The purpose of this chapter is to help you argue and plan for high-quality music in a cross-curricular context. Equally important, but not contradictory, this chapter also constitutes a plea for the retention of the unique insights and disciplined skills, knowledge and understandings of a distinct music curriculum.

OBJECTIVES

By the end of this chapter you should be able to:

- argue for the creative input of music in cross-curricular projects;
- plan for appropriate musical inputs to cross-curricular projects;
- understand the difference between interdisciplinary, multidisciplinary and chance uses of music within cross-curricular projects;
- differentiate between when music is best learned in a stand-alone context or together with other subjects.

MUSIC, CREATIVITY AND OTHER DISCIPLINES

Music is inherently creative and creative outcomes are particularly evident in cross-arts projects. Box 10.1 contains examples of a range of creative cross-arts projects involving music which were completed over the course of a year in a single performing arts college for pupils aged 11–18.

> **Box 10.1   Examples of creative cross-arts projects**
>
> A *photographic/projection project*: collecting images of students learning which was then beamed onto the windows of a school building to the soundtrack of improvised music recorded by pupils.
>
> *Lovely Bones*: a musical score which arose from the story of the book of the same name and was performed as a dramatised reading to music. Pupils assessed its effectiveness by how far it enhanced the understanding of the story.
>
> *Punk28*: an improvisation session which grew into a cross-arts collaboration. A recording was used as the basis for a composition process as the piece was shaped, refined, quantised and produced to accompany a dance and movement display for parents and friends of the college.
>
> *The Royal Opera House (ROH) project*: where year 7 pupils worked intensively with singers and players from the ROH to produce their own mini opera on playground issues. This project involved the combined dance, drama, art and music staff, who agreed that they learned as much as the pupils.

Creativity might be defined as the collision of two ideas to make a valued new one (Koestler 1967). Task 10.1 describes how it may be possible to illustrate creative thinking in music when colliding with another subject discipline. It introduces a simple and highly transferable exercise in creative music-making which starts with a creative writing exercise.

> **Task 10.1   Musical Haikus**
>
> Each student teacher should write their own Haiku (a Japanese poetry form consisting at its simplest of three lines – five syllables, seven syllables and five syllables) about a small and insignificant part of their local environment, such as a crumpled leaf, a sweet wrapper or an abandoned coffee cup.
>
> In groups of five, share the Haikus and choose one Haiku which could best be put to a musical accompaniment. The group then uses instruments, voices and/or found sounds to compose a musical backing or replacement for the chosen Haiku. Student teachers can use the words of the Haiku repeated, patterned, emphasised or used simply as musical sound to make their music. The music could be composed to suggest the 'feeling' generated by the words and replace them entirely. The following framework should be given.
>
> The music should:
> - start from the ideas generated by the Haiku;
> - be about one minute long;
> - use voices, instruments and/or found sounds;
> - fully involve all five group members;
> - avoid simple 'sound effects'.
>
> What do you observe about the relationship between the words and the music?

MUSIC, LEARNING AND OTHER DISCIPLINES

Contemporary cross-curricular studies are characterised by the use of two or more perspectives to make sense of a single theme or experience. Research strongly suggests that cross-curricular approaches stimulate strong engagement on the part of pupils and teachers but that *minimising* the number of subject approaches is the most effective way of ensuring subject progression in a cross-curricular context (Wineburg and Grossman 2000). However, combining two subjects does not automatically result in learning in both or either.

Before making progress in using cross-curricular methods you need to be confident about what is distinctive about music. We are reminded in the NC to consider music in its performing, composing, reviewing and evaluating contexts and to help pupils become aware of the significance of time, space and culture. It is important to reiterate these well-known directions, because if cross-curricular music is *not* expanding pupils' understanding of one or more of these things, then it is not fulfilling a musically important purpose. Skills and knowledge in music may be progressively enriched either by teaching them first and asking pupils to apply them in a new situation later or by allowing the need for skills and knowledge to arise directly from an activity.

Specifically, a few examples will illustrate the kinds of musical skills and knowledge which can be developed through cross-curricular work. Collaborative arts projects, for example, can often have the effect of deepening pupils' understanding of the meaning of music itself. 'It's like I have discovered a new world of music that I never knew existed', said one year 9 pupil after a project where her class composed music to accompany a Channel Tunnel rail trip (Creative Partnerships Kent (CP) 2006: 46). A year 12 dance pupil spoke of the 'fresh way of thinking and creating movement material' working with a professional musician had brought to her work (CP 2006: 40).

Try Task 10.2 with pupils to show how simple musical structures like rondo form can be used to link disparate episodes of composed music. If it is linked to a real journey and to the development of skills such as mapping and direction finding in geography, it will illustrate how a single experience can bring about learning in two disciplines.

Task 10.2   Musical journeys

Ask each individual pupil to take a short journey with a 'journey stick' (a 15cm strip of card with a strip of double-sided sticky tape attached). They should be directed to collect five tiny objects which catch their eye on their journey and stick them onto their 'journey stick'. On return to class they should make a sketch map of their journey with symbols to represent where they found each of their objects. Their musical challenge is to turn their five objects into five musical episodes and compose a linking theme to represent the route of their journey.

- What specific musical learning arises out of this task?

The built environment can also be used as a powerful starting point for cross-curricular learning. In the case study in Box 10.2 pupils can be led to discuss the range of subject-based responses which arise from a nearby building. The musical response to such a stimulus is summarised below.

Box 10.2 Structure in music

Pupils find a nearby building or section of building. They mentally (or in a drawing) divide the building into its main sections; either left to right (e.g. wall, window, wall, door, wall, window, wall) or bottom to top (e.g. grass, wall, windows, wall, windows, wall, windows, wall, roof). The sections are represented by letters (e.g. wall = A, window = B, door = C). The pupils compose separate musics to represent window, door and wall which then can be performed in the sequence suggested by the building. The building is 'read' like a graphic score. Its symmetry (or asymmetry) will have helped to provide a distinctive structure to the composed music.

APPROACHES TO CROSS-CURRICULAR WORK

A range of approaches to cross-curricular work may be adopted. It is possible to combine musical approaches intricately with another subject in response to a stimulus and this can be called an interdisciplinary approach. When musical and other subject responses arise from a single stimulus but remain essentially separate, then this can be called a multi-disciplinary approach. Some cross-curricular work will arise by chance.

Interdisciplinary approaches to cross-curricularity

Music can be an equal partner in responding to a single powerful experience. The simultaneous application of musical knowledge and skills and those of other disciplines are common in the arts and advertising. Apart from school productions, such combinations of disciplines are a growing, but not common, curriculum experience. If we examine the ways in which music is used in popular culture, TV, film, video games, promotional or advertising videos and DVDs, we hear it used as background, but composed in highly sophisticated ways which take full account of the listener, the intended mood, the context and the subtleties of movement and narrative. In other words, knowledge of certain musical structures; sequences, cycles of fifths, ostinati, pedal notes, repetitions and so on, are used to enhance the emotional power of the image. The music is less comprehensible without the image and the image less affecting without the music; both have equal and complementary status.

Box 10.3 Film and music

Year 8 pupils in a London secondary school used an internet advertising clip for the film *Polar Express* (www.imdb.com/video/screenplay/vi1475477785/) to stimulate composition. The media studies and music teachers team taught two consecutive sessions using this clip. Using media studies skills they examined how the clip drew them in and made them want to borrow the DVD from the local store. The commercially composed music played a major part in this analysis. The music teacher explained in the same session how timbre, dynamics and musical sequence helped create this compelling atmosphere. Pupils were then set the challenge of making an alternative score to accompany the clip. The restrictions of precise timing, limited music technology or instruments and quickly changing scenes provided a challenging frame for groups of pupils to work within.

The challenge in the case study in Box 10.3 was real, relevant and possible, though pupils had never tackled such a test before. The teachers reported that all members of the group appeared in a state of what psychologist Csikszentmihalyi (2002) calls 'flow' – that state where the activity is *so* engaging that time, present worries and self-consciousness all become unimportant. In this flow state many groups asked to continue the activity through break time and said at the end that time had passed very quickly. Now carry out Task 10.3.

Task 10.3 Soundtrack: film and music

Choose an appropriate video clip from YouTube or www.imdb.com. Mute the sound controls and set a task to compose a soundtrack for the clip. The music must be exactly the same length as the clip and music must be decided upon to add to the visual impact of the film. Present group compositions together with the video images.

- Discuss the impact of (a) the exercise itself on the student teachers, (b) the music on perceptions of the video clip.

In such interdisciplinary approaches music has an equal standing with other subjects.

Multidisciplinary approaches to cross-curricularity

Cross-curricular work where subjects remain independent within a shared theme may be called a *multi*disciplinary approach. There are advantages to the stand-alone quality inherent in our definition of multidisciplinary learning. Progressive development of skills, knowledge and attitudes may be more carefully introduced, controlled and monitored while maintaining the motivating aspects of a thematic curriculum. The integrity of music can more easily be preserved and products may be more refined. Lastly, music may be honoured specifically for its contribution to human understanding. However, there are disadvantages too. In a multidisciplinary approach, creativity may be more difficult to engender because unexpected links are less often made.

Musically creative ideas, however, are very possible when pupils are confident in simply playing with sound. A musical response to a theme like 'water' may influence the kinds of questions a scientist asks about it. When pupils and teachers begin to ask real, relevant, original and subject-based questions they are acting like experts in the discipline. Perhaps when we (teachers or pupils) put on the mantle of 'the expert', creative (original, values, imaginative) responses are much more likely.

A cross-curricular day or week around a theme like 'water' might generate subject-based responses which are entirely independent of each other but all related to a single starting point. The case study in Box 10.4 exemplifies this.

Box 10.4 Our town

In year 9 of a Kent Academy, perspectives from Geography, Psychology and Music were applied to a study of the local streets. Pupils first used a ground plan of the streets surrounding their school to create an *emotional map* of the area. In small groups and in different streets they adopted their own categories and key to plot areas they felt were *threatening, safe, peaceful, boring, interesting* and so on. In class they debated why various

---

Box 10.4 *continued*

feelings were common to particular areas of their town and any implications which arose. In their music sessions they revisited the streets and, using acoustic percussion and some orchestral instruments, made musical representations of key spots on their journey: the street, the view of the sea, the tower block, the playing fields, the back alley and the main road.

In the case study in Box 10.4 pupils were highly motivated to participate. One pupil said he had never seen his own locality as worth thinking about and many said they had changed their views on the place. Because music was treated separately within the wider theme, the music teacher was able to support pupils in carefully selecting appropriate timbres through listening to different acoustic effects. She was able to raise the bar of the challenge by teaching about *theme and variations* form which musically expressed the basic houses in the estate which had been elaborated by porches, leaded windows, elaborate gardens and expressive paintwork. Pupils soon noticed that this was a structure that could be repeated in their 'sea view' compositions. The pupils became so involved in these compositions that the project continued for longer than the teacher had planned and eventually became part of a mapping exhibition mounted in the school hall at the end of term.

Task 10.4 will allow you to explore another multidisciplinary approach.

Task 10.4 Out and about around our school

Plan a three-week unit of work which starts with a short walk around the locality of the school with a simple base map. Groups of pupils collect information on such aspects as function, wear and tear, noise pollution, traffic, type of building. For the musical aspect of this locality study, pupils are given support (in the form of taught sessions on musical timbre and texture) to compose pieces inspired by the mood of different parts of the locality, the functions of particular shops, or textures or patterns found in a range of buildings. Compositions are presented as part of an exhibition on the locality for parents and governors.

Music by chance

Music may arise from any open and enquiring interaction with an environment, theme or issue. Sometimes for the teacher a musical response comes unplanned and unexpected. A music teacher who is beginning to think like a professional composer or performer can capture these moments and build them into opportunities to develop musical understandings in a variety of ways. The extended case study in Box 10.5 outlines an example where musical responses happened more by chance than intention.

Box 10.5 Case study: the 'essence' of a place

In what was known as the HEARTS (Higher Education, Arts and Schools) project, pupils from year 7 at a coastal community college and a group of student teachers were dropped at a wide and windswept shingle beach in mid-November. The forlorn beach was dominated by two giant power stations, pylons, scattered huts, fishing boats and gulls. The combined groups had only one instruction – to 'capture the essence' of this place. Pupils and student teachers used digital recorders, cameras, mobile phones, note books and discarded plastic bags to collect the essence of the beach. Returning to school with a collection of digital recordings, images and flotsam, students and pupils had to work on constructing some kind of presentation which would express their experience to the rest of their year group. Many chose musical composition as a powerful way of capturing their encounter with isolation, wind, rain, nuclear power and pebbles.

Pupils and student teachers worked together to construct a series of five-minute presentations. Some groups manipulated and refined their recorded sounds of the crashing waves, wind in the electric wires, gulls circling above and pebbles moving underfoot. Over a pre-recorded drone of manipulated wave sounds, one group improvised gull shrieks using three dismembered soprano recorders, while a single pupil created acoustic sound using a bass drum and a scrubbing brush. The remainder of the group made shapes with their bodies which melted from one grisly shape to the next in a repeated dance capturing the salt-tolerant plants which clung to the pebbles.

Using a sound manipulation programme such as Audacity, another group transformed their simple recording of pebbles into a crescendo of angular sounds which filled the school hall and then suddenly stopped. They repeated this block of sound three times to represent the monolithic structures of the power station on the beach. In seeking to refine the impact of the sound, students and pupils worked hard to preserve as much internal variation of sound as possible. On their ten-second recording they separated the impact and decay sounds of stones hitting each other and the high and low sounds of pebbles sliding over each other. They used echo, reverberation and reverse functions to create six separate tracks of sound from their tiny sample. Pupils decided that placing groups of three shattering sounds on a loop divided by a space of 60 seconds would be enough to provide an atmosphere which truly arose from the place when visitors walked along a line of paintings of aspects of the beach contributed by each member of the team. On hearing presentations from others one member of this group suggested a continuous high-pitched pedal note to link their 'sound monuments' which was included at the last minute.

(Barnes and Shirley 2007)

The teachers using this open-ended cross-curricular activity had opportunities to provide focused support for pupils when they needed it. In the course of their responses to an authentic and strong stimulus pupils learned, with help from more able peers, teachers and technicians, to manipulate sound using technology and place it in the context of a simple musical structure. The motivation and desire for such musical development arose from the enthusiasm generated by a chance discovery at a beach. Task 10.5 takes the HEARTS idea and translates it to a location on the campus, for example, a car park, fence, pond, dining hall or library.

> **Task 10.5** A special place
>
> Working with four or five other student teachers, visit a number of particular and contrasting locations around your university or college campus. Focus on detail in the place, e.g. draw a spot where two contrasting materials meet, list the connections or feelings which arise in the mind while reflecting on the place, etc. Think about what makes 'your' place unique and special. Your task is to make a presentation to the rest of the group which captures the essence of your place. It must include a sonic response which has been generated in some way by your interaction with the place.

By capturing a special place with sound and other responses you will inevitably and unpredictably combine a number of subject disciplines. It may take some time to refine responses into an acceptable performance. Formative assessment during the process can both model and support good practice in teaching and learning. For example, partly formed presentations can be presented in an unpolished form *before* the final performance. This will give opportunities to give focused and formative feedback, ask questions and perhaps suggest improvements.

SUMMARY

There are three distinct ways of using music in a cross-curricular way. It is possible to combine musical approaches intricately with another subject in response to a stimulus and this can be called interdisciplinary learning. When musical and other subject responses arise from a single stimulus but remain essentially separate, then this may be seen as a multidisciplinary approach. Musical responses may also arise from a chance discovery during a strong personal and shared experience such as a trip to the beach, theatre or the visit of a team of experts. Each of these approaches is cross-curricular and can be of equal value to the musical development of children.

There are times, however, when music is best taught alone. When new skills and knowledge need to be established, the distraction of other ways of thinking can easily confuse both teacher and pupil. There are times when music easily and powerfully integrates with other subject disciplines to provide multiple understandings of an issue. The secret for teachers is to know when to use which approach. Teachers may prefer to use separate music sessions to teach the disciplined skills and knowledge of music and then *quickly* give pupils the opportunity to apply that knowledge and those skills within an authentic, relevant and cross-curricular challenge. Others may see musical development happening in parallel with creative engagement in projects. In cross-curricular contexts music may stand alone in a multidisciplined study making its response to a theme, question or problem to support understanding of wider themes. Musical skills and knowledge, once established, may also be closely intertwined with one or two other subjects (particularly arts) to provide the rounded understanding typical of real-world learning.

FURTHER READING

Creative Partnerships: www.creative-partnerships.com/
A government-funded organisation which works with some of the most deprived communities in the UK spearheading whole school change through long-term creative and cross-curricular projects.

Qualifications and Curriculum Authority: http://curriculum.qca.org.uk/
The Creativity section of the QCA website gives practical ideas on how to promote pupils' creative thinking and behaviour.

Royal Opera House: http://info.royaloperahouse.org/Education/Index.cfm
An example of a website devoted to promoting school–culture links at the highest level of professional and educational practice.

Sound Station: www.thesoundstation.org.uk/jsp/SS_Home.jsp
Sound Station is linked with Youth Music.

Youth Music: www.youthmusic.org.uk/
Government-funded Youth Music helps fund many community and education schemes throughout the UK.

References

Assessment Reform Group (ARG) (2002) *Assessment for Learning: 10 Principles*. London: ARG. Available at http://k1.ioe.ac.uk/tlrp/arg/publications.html (accessed 28 November 2008).

Barnes, J. and Shirley, I. (2005) Promoting Creativity in Initial Teacher Education: a study by tutors and students at Canterbury Christ Church University involved in the 'HEARTS project' in a paper presented to the British Educational Research Association Annual Conference, University of Glamorgan, 14–17 September.

Barnes, J. and Shirley, I. (2007) 'Strangely familiar: cross curricular and creative thinking in teacher education', *Improving Schools*, 10(2): 289–306.

Bauman, Z. (2000) *Liquid Modernity*. Cambridge: Polity Press.

Black, P. and Wiliam, D. (2006) 'Assessment for learning in the classroom', in J. Gardner (ed.) *Assessment and Learning*. London: Sage.

Black, P., Harrison, C., Lee, C., Marshall, B. and Wiliam, D. (2003) *Assessment for Learning: Putting It into Practice*. Maidenhead: Open University Press.

Bloom, B.S. (1956) *Taxonomy of Educational Objectives. Handbook I: The Cognitive Domain*. New York: David McKay.

Central Advisory Council for Education (1967) *Children and their Primary Schools* (Plowden Report). London: HMSO.

Coll, H. (2007) 'Transition in music education', in C. Philpott and G. Spruce (eds) *Learning to Teach Music in the Secondary School*, 2nd edn. London: RoutledgeFalmer.

Craft, A. (2005) *Creativity in Schools: Tensions and Dilemmas*. London: Routledge.

Creative Partnerships Kent (2006) *Footnotes to an Idea*. London: Arts Council.

Crow, B. (2007) 'Music related ICT in education', in C. Philpott and G. Spruce (eds) *Learning to Teach Music in the Secondary School*, 2nd edn. London: RoutledgeFalmer.

Csikszentmihalyi, M. (2002) *Flow: The Classic Work on How to Achieve Happiness*. London: Rider.

Day, C. (2004) *A Passion for Teaching*. London: RoutledgeFalmer.

Department for Children, Schools and Families (DCSF) (2008) *Guidance on the Music Standards Fund Grant 1.11 2008–2011*. London: The Stationery Office.

Department for Education and Skills (DfES) (2001) *Schools Achieving Success*. London: DfES.

Department for Education and Skills (DfES) (2006a) *Music Manifesto Report no. 2: Making Every Child's Music Matter*. London: The Stationery Office.

Department for Education and Skills (DfES) (2006b) *2020 Vision: Report of the Teaching and Learning in 2020 Review Group*. London: DfES.

Edexcel (2007) *Specification 2007 GCE Music*. Available at www.edexcel.com/quals/gce/gce08/music/music/Pages/default.aspx (accessed 22 November 2008).

Edexcel (2008) *Edexcel GCSE in Music (2MU01) Specification*. London: Edexcel. Available at www.edexcel.com/quals/gcse/gcse09/music/Pages/default.aspx (assessed 28 November 2008).

Fautley, M. (2008) *Assessment in Music Education: Questions and Answers (NAME Information Bulletin 1/08)*. Matlock, Derbyshire: National Association of Music Educators.

Fautley, M. and Savage, J. (2007) *Creativity in Secondary Education*. Exeter: Learning Matters.

Green, L. (2001) *How Popular Musicians Learn*. Aldershot: Ashgate.

Green, L. (2002) 'Research in the sociology of music education', in G. Spruce (ed.) *Teaching Music in Secondary Schools: A Reader*. London: The Open University.

Green, L. (2008) *Music, Informal Learning and the School: A New Classroom Pedagogy*. Aldershot: Ashgate.

Hallam, S., Creech, A., Rogers, L. and Papageorgi, I. (2007) *Local Authority Music Services Provision 2007 for Key Stages 1 and 2. Research Report DCFS-RR014*. London: Department for Children, Schools and Families.

Hargreaves, D.H. (2006) *A New Shape for Schooling*. London: Specialist School and Academies Trust.

Harlen, W. (2006) 'On the relationship between assessment for formative and summative purposes', in J. Gardner (ed.) *Assessment and Learning*. London: Sage.

Harlen, W. and James, M. (1997) 'Assessment and learning: differences and relationships between formative and summative assessments', *Assessment in Education*, 4(3): 365–379.

Jameson, F. (1998) *The Cultural Turn: Selected Writings on the Postmodern, 1983–1988*. London: Verso.

Koestler, A. (1967) *The Act of Creation*. London: Dell.

Lewis, S. (2005) 'Drumming, silence and making it up', in P. Moser and G. McKay (eds) *Community Music: A Handbook*. Lyme Regis: Russell House.

Marshall, N. and Hargreaves, D. (2007) 'Crossing the humpback bridge: primary–secondary school transition in music education', *British Journal of Music Education*, 9(1): 65–80.

Mills, J. (1996) 'Starting at secondary school', *British Journal of Music Education*, 13(1): 5–14.

Mills, J. (2007) *Instrumental Teaching*. Oxford: Oxford University Press.

Moser, P. and McKay, G. (eds) (2005) *Community Music: A Handbook*. Lyme Regis: Russell House.

National Curriculum Council (NCC) (1990) *The Arts 5–16: A Curriculum Framework*. London: Oliver & Boyd.

OCR (2008) *OCR AS/A level GCE Music version 2 – February 2008 specification*. Available at www.ocr.org.uk/qualifications/asa_levelgceforfirstteachingin2008/music/index.html (accessed 22 November 2008).

Ofsted (2003) *Good Assessment Practice in Music* (HMI Document 1479). London: Ofsted.

Ofsted (2005) *2004/05 Annual Report of Her Majesty's Chief Inspector of Schools*. London: The Stationery Office.

Orfali, A. (2004) *Artists Working in Partnership with Schools*. Newcastle upon Tyne: Arts Council England, North East.

Paterson, A. and Davies, L. (eds) (2005) *Rites of Passage: Effective Transition and Curriculum Continuity in Music Education*. Matlock, Derbyshire: National Association of Music Educators.

Philpott, C. (2007a) 'Assessment in music education', in C. Philpott and G. Spruce (eds) *Learning to Teach Music in the Secondary School*, 2nd edn. London: RoutledgeFalmer.

Philpott, C. (2007b) *What is Musical Learning? Key Stage 2 Music CPD*. The Open University and Trinity Guildhall.

Philpott, C. and Spruce, G. (eds) (2007) *Learning to Teach Music in the Secondary School: A Companion to School Experience*, 2nd edn. London: RoutledgeFalmer.

Price, D. (2007) *Musical Futures: From Vision to Practice*. London: Paul Hamlyn Foundation.

Qualifications and Curriculum Authority (QCA) (2005) *Music: 2004/5 Annual Report on Curriculum and Assessment*. London: QCA. Available at www.qca.org.uk/qca_10236.aspx (accessed 22 November 2008).

Qualifications and Curriculum Authority (2007a) *GCSE Subject Criteria for Music*. London: QCA.

Qualifications and Curriculum Authority (2007b) *Music: Programme of Study for Key Stage 3 and Attainment Target*. London: QCA.

Qualifications and Curriculum Authority (2007c) *National Curriculum for Music Key Stage 3*. London: QCA. Available at http://curriculum.qca.org.uk/key-stages-3-and-4/subjects/music/index.aspx (accessed 22 November 2008).

Sadler, D. (1989) 'Formative assessment and the design of instructional systems', *Instructional Science*, 18: 119–144.

Savage, J. (2007) 'Is musical performance worth saving? The importance of musical performance in teaching and learning', in C. Philpott and G. Spruce (eds) *Learning to Teach Music in the Secondary School*, 2nd edn. London: RoutledgeFalmer.

Schmidt, P. (2005) 'Music education as transformative practice: creating new frameworks for learning music through a Freirian perspective', *Visions of Research in Music Education* (special edition), January.

School Curriculum and Assessment Authority (SCAA) (1996) *Key Stage 3 Optional Tests and Tasks – Music Unit 2: Musical Ideas*. Hayes, Middlesex: SCAA Publications.

Swanwick, K. (1988) *Music, Mind, and Education*. London: Routledge.

Thompson, E.P. (1993) *Customs in Common: Studies in Traditional Popular Culture*. New York: The New Press.

Wallas, W. (1926) *Art of Thought*. New York: Harcourt Brace.

Webster, A., Beveridge, M. and Reed, M. (1995) *Managing the Literacy Curriculum*. London: Routledge.

Williams, R. (1980) *The Long Revolution*. London: Penguin.

Willis, P. (1990) *Moving Culture*. London: Calouste Gulbenkian Foundation.

Wineburg, S. and Grossman, P. (2000) *Interdisciplinary Curriculum: Challenges to Implementation*. New York: Teachers College Press.

Winterson, J. (2002) *50 Music Assignments for the BTEC First Diploma*. London: Peters.

Woodford, P. (2005) *Democracy and Music Education: Liberalism, Ethics, and the Politics of Practice*. Bloomington, IN: Indiana University Press.

Zwozdiak-Myers, P. and Capel, S. (2005) 'Communicating with pupils', in S. Capel, M. Leask and T. Turner (eds) *Learning to Teach in the Secondary School*, 4th edn. London: Routledge.

Index